Cycling for Women

by the editors of *Bicycling*® magazine

Rodale Press, Emmaus, Pennsylvania

Printed in the United States of America on acid-free paper containing a high percentage of recycled fiber.

Edited by Kim Anderson

Library of Congress Cataloging-in-Publication Data

Cycling for women.

   1. Cycling for women.   I. Bicycling.
GV1057.C93   1989   796.6'024042   88-31813
ISBN 0-87857-811-0   paperback

2 4 6 8 10 9 7 5 3 1   paperback

Contents

Contents

Introduction

by Connie Carpenter Phinney,
Gold Medalist, 1984 Olympic Road Race

Traditionally, women have shied away from serious cycling. The mechanics of the bike, the physical demands of the sport, and the uniqueness of the clothing combined to act as deterrents. But times are changing and more women are riding.

When you think about it, the bicycle is a great equalizer. Every body type fits a bicycle and any person, regardless of age or sex, can excel on one. In fact, a smart woman can be competitive against a stronger man simply by using common sense and intuition. But being competitive doesn't necessarily mean wanting to win races.

I remember a woman who attended the training camp my husband (7-Eleven team pro Davis Phinney) and I hold every summer at Colorado's Copper Mountain Resort. Her goal had nothing to do with real races – she wanted to beat her boyfriend on one of their favorite training rides. She was a talented cyclist and no doubt gave him a run for his money.

It may sound unreasonable but the one goal I never achieved as a competitive cyclist was to win a top level men's race. Even though many men in Colorado, where I live and trained, gauged their progress by how well they did in comparison to me, I never finished better than fourth. This happened in a race in Aspen. Alexi Grewal (1984 Olympic road race champion) won.

Actually, I started cycling only after being forced from competitive speed skating by an injury in 1976. I had ridden a bike for summer training and had been exposed to the sport by my older brother Chuck (a racer) and by Sheila Young, a former world champion in speed skating and cycling. But in my first competitive season I exceeded even my wildest expectations, winning two national titles. Yet my most vivid memory is not of that year's National Championships but of a club race in my hometown of Madison, Wisconsin.

Since few women raced in '76, these weekly events usually had me pitted against the men. In this race, I was in the lead with my training partner and good friend, Ben Caldwell. At 6 feet 5 inches, Ben didn't have the ideal body type for cycling, but it was perfect for breaking the wind. I clung to his wheel, and as we came out of the last turn we sprinted for the finish. Ben thought he had me, but he fumbled a gear change and I won. My reward came that night when his four male roommates called to congratulate me. This was a sport I could learn to like!

Eight years, hundreds of races, and thousands of miles later, I had realized my loftiest goal in cycling – winning the 1984 Olympic road race.

When I jumped from that podium in Los Angeles, I jumped into my second career – working as a free-lance writer, television and radio commentator, and cycling consultant. I knew little about the business world and, having lived in the sheltered upper echelon of the racing establishment, I wasn't sure if I'd fit in. But the self-confidence I built while cycling gave me courage in this unfamiliar territory. The lessons I learned, especially while competing against men, gave me insight and competence in a male-dominated world. Although winning is less tangible, I simply applied the tactics of bicycle racing to business.

Besides creating new pressures, my career affords me little time for riding. Instead of cycling every day, I find it is a luxury to ride three times a week. And those rides I once took for granted, ones that used to be easy, are now much more difficult. Yet I've discovered that I enjoy recreational riding.

I also discovered something else – that many fit women give little thought to racing. They seem content to ride recreationally. Once, a particularly strong woman cyclist passed me during a charity ride in California. She apologized. When I was in racing, apology was not part of the game. This was a new etiquette. The enthusiasm with which these recreational riders attacked the road also surprised me. In fact, it's infectious, and after almost a decade of racing I've been born again as a recreational rider.

Cycling is, after all, a sport for everyone. For women, it can be particularly rewarding because it puts us in command and in control. Improvement is easy; it simply takes practice. Success is measured by miles ridden and terrain overcome. It's a sport that's simultaneously exhilarating and grueling. The experience of any ride varies from elation to frustration, but the result is always satisfying.

To accept the challenge of the road is to take a journey inside yourself. How many times have you said you couldn't climb a hill or keep the pace, and then done it? Or – if you did give up – remember the regret you felt afterward?

A few years ago I crossed 12,000-foot Independence Pass in Colorado with 1,400 cyclists. Although most doubted their abilities at the start, everyone made it to the top. And it will be easier for them next time. Meeting such challenges not only gives you immediate satisfaction, but it also imparts a self-confidence that extends into other areas of your life. Success breeds success.

There is no limit to the challenges cycling offers. There are always other roads to ride and more hills to climb. Cycling is more than a way of life: It's a way of improving the *quality* of your life.

Part One
The Facts about Women and Cycling

Can a Woman Be
an Exceptional Cyclist?

Women and cycling go back a long way. The invention of the bicycle in the mid-1800s actually gave females entrance into the world of recreational sport. Once-sedate ladies enthusiastically embraced the new activity (although "proper" citizens were scandalized, claiming it was lewd, indecorous, sinful, and bound to result in illicit sex and miscarriages). Women hitched up their skirts, pinned back their hair, and reveled in an independence and physical exhilaration they had rarely known.

Today, women and cycling coexist pleasantly. In fact, a recent survey by the Bicycle Federation of America indicates that more women are cycling than men. Statistics also show that most new riders are women, that race times for women are dropping steadily, that manufacturers are marketing a record number of goods designed for female cyclists, and that the level of sophistication about bicycling among women is growing.

But without belaboring the obvious, female cyclists remain fundamentally different from their male counterparts. As a result, they face unique obstacles and enjoy unique advantages – some physical, some psychological, and some societal. To become the best cyclist possible, each woman should understand these differences along with the limitations and benefits they impart.

Differences in Design

The most obvious difference between men and women is physique. The average American woman is 5 feet 4 inches and

125 pounds. The average American man is 5 feet 8 inches, 154 pounds. Women tend to have longer legs, shorter arms, and a lower center of gravity than men. None of these differences overly help or hinder a woman rider, as long as her bike is properly fitted.

But several unique aspects of a woman's body *will* affect her cycling significantly. For example, because women have less muscle mass and more essential fat than men, they're usually not as strong and have more inert mass. Typically, a sedentary college-age man is 15 percent fat and 49 percent muscle. His female counterpart is 27 percent fat and 36 percent muscle. This discrepancy is found even among elite cyclists, where the men typically average 8 percent body fat and the women, 15 percent.

Photograph 1-1. A woman's bicycle has to reflect the unique characteristics of her body.

Three to 5 percent is usually identified as a man's essential fat level (the minimum he must maintain to avoid health problems). A woman's essential fat level is generally higher – about 8 percent. Women require more fat than men because they bear children. In fact, prepubescent boys and girls have similar body compositions. Only after puberty do differences appear. Males add prodigious amounts of new muscle to their bodies, while women typically add fat. It is by no means unattractive or nonfunctional, however: Fat gives a woman her shape, the fullness of breasts and hips. This fat may also be necessary for childbearing, outfitting the potential mother with a storehouse of nourishment.

Nevertheless, fat isn't much of an advantage for cyclists. Researchers once speculated that having large fat reserves might make a woman a better endurance athlete, since she would have access to more stored calories. This theory has since been disproven.

"There is no basis for the notion that women can mobilize or utilize fat any better than men," says Christine Wells, Ph.D., a professor of exercise physiology at Arizona State University.

In fact, women may be at a disadvantage. Like men, they first use muscle glycogen for fuel. But because they generally eat less than men, these stores are lower. Furthermore, according to some researchers, the female hormone estrogen may limit the muscles' ability to warehouse glycogen.

The key difference between a man's and woman's performance, however, involves the maximum amount of oxygen that each can deliver to their muscles during exercise. Called VO_2 max, this is perhaps the best indicator of potential success in endurance events. Because women usually have smaller hearts and lungs and less blood than men, the average woman's VO_2 max is 12 to 15 percent lower. Thus, it takes more effort to match a man's speed over a given distance.

Does all this mean a woman's physiology precludes her from being a successful cyclist? Hardly, says Dr. Wells. "As more women undertake serious conditioning and training, I believe many former physiological barriers will fall by the wayside."

Recent studies have also shown that female bicycle racers have less body fat and higher VO_2 max than inactive men. In fact, the VO_2 max of national-class female cyclists is generally higher than that of professional tennis, baseball, and ice hockey players.

Cycling through Your Cycle

Women were once urged to avoid exercising (and even to avoid polite company) during "certain times of the month." A woman was thought to be more delicate and less stable during her period. Studies have since prompted researchers to think otherwise.

"Women may have been socialized to believe they are somehow too fragile to exercise vigorously, especially during their period," says Diane Wakat, Ph.D., professor of health education at the University of Virginia.

But science does not support this belief. For example, the production of lactic acid (a substance in the muscles that inhibits performance) is no greater during menstruation and the numbers prove that women – including cyclists – have managed to set records and win Olympic medals during all phases of their cycle.

Still, many women feel tired or less enthusiastic about their workouts at specific times each month. Such fatigue or malaise varies widely from woman to woman and science can't readily account for it. But for those who experience it, doctors usually recommend charting cycles for several months and noting those times when you're least inspired to exercise. Then, simply plan to train lightly or avoid racing on those days.

If menstrual cramping interferes with your cycling, there are remedies. The nonprescription drug ibuprofen (contained in Nuprin, Advil, Motrin, Trendar, and Midol IB) will minimize cramping – so much so, according to Dr. Wakat, that you should be able to exercise without difficulty shortly after taking the recommended dosage.

While menstruation should have little effect on your cycling, there is some debate as to what cycling can do to your period. Some doctors have claimed that strenuous training will disrupt a woman's cycle, interfering with her fertility and possibly her health. In certain cases, women athletes have stopped having their periods, a condition known as amenorrhea. It won't permanently affect your ability to become pregnant, but amenorrhea may influence how your body stores calcium. No period means little or no estrogen production, and estrogen is essential for calcium storage. Amenorrheic women are consequently thought to be at greater risk of developing osteoporosis.

But the connection between exercise and amenorrhea has never been proven. "Do athletes become amenorrheic because they are athletes or because of other factors?" asks Anne Loucks, Ph.D., assistant research endocrinologist at the University of California in San Diego.

"Women athletes tend to be thin. They tend to shun certain foods. They may be anxious about competition. The so-called 'athletic lifestyle' may contribute more to the development of amenorrhea than the actual exercise."

Likewise, the ramifications of the condition itself are also suspect. "The prevailing explanation of amenorrhea has defined it as a disease," says one doctor, "whereas our research indicates it is an adaptation and a perfectly healthy one. If a woman athlete is amenorrheic now but wants to become pregnant later, she can. Her reproductive system has not changed permanently."

It's reassuring to note that in most studies, the athletes who developed menstrual irregularities were serious runners. Few cyclists had problems. But if your period does change, either after you begin riding or after you increase your mileage, see a doctor – preferably a gynecologist who is familiar with athletic amenorrhea.

Outsprinting Stereotypes

The greatest barrier women face in their attempt to become serious cyclists, says Chuck Corbin, Ph.D., a professor of physical education and exercise science at Arizona State University, is not biological, but psychological.

"In athletics, women generally have much less confidence than men," he explains. "This has one of two effects. It causes women to avoid sports altogether or do less well than they could, out of fear of failing."

Dr. Corbin attributes this lack of confidence to the minimal amount of support society has traditionally given female athletes.

"If a task of any kind is perceived as somehow sex-specific, then society will discourage people of the opposite sex from participating. This has been the case with women and sports.

Women have been discouraged from taking part in anything that involves strength, speed, contact or aggression. . . . Competitive cycling has long been considered unfeminine. And it is this image that has kept many women from participating."

Even those women who do participate in competitive sports such as cycling may be handicapped by the way they were raised. "Young boys grow up playing aggressively against one another," says Dr. Corbin. "They learn very early how to evaluate their progress and their own abilities in comparison to their friends. Most young women don't. [As a result] women not only worry about doing something unfeminine, but they also worry about doing it badly. They worry they can't or maybe shouldn't perform well. Such an attitude almost guarantees failure. A woman goes out with low expectations, can't evaluate whether she's doing well, decides she isn't, and quits the sport."

Photograph 1-2. Pure pleasure is a good enough reason to start cycling.

But Dr. Corbin insists that a woman *can* build confidence and, in this case, become a successful cyclist. At first, he recommends riding without goals – cycling for the pure pleasure of it. Then – but only after you've developed into a capable rider – start setting specific training goals.

"At this point, it helps to work with an understanding friend," Dr. Corbin suggests. "This person should help you learn to evaluate your progress honestly and on your own. He or she should ask, 'How do you think you just did?' Then, together you should evaluate your opinion of yourself and how it compares to the more objective view.

"You should learn not to undervalue your abilities and achievements. If you always predict you'll do less well than you're capable of doing, you're not being modest or ladylike – you're just protecting yourself from failure. And you're guaranteeing that you'll never really succeed.

"We need to change our definition of feminine," he adds. "Feminine behavior is whatever a woman does. If she cycles well, if she races aggressively, she's being feminine in her own way and on her own terms. I, for one, think that's great."

Five Myths

Myth 1: Riding hard will make me more tense. You arrive home from work feeling tired, tense, and irritable. Your job is the source of the stress, but your family compounds it. What's the best way to ease the pounding in your head and relax tight muscles? The answer, according to new research: Ride hard.

Strenuous cycling reduces tension more effectively than riding at a leisurely pace, according to Robert Bulbulian, Ph.D., and Martha Ebert, R.N., M.S., of the University of Kentucky's exercise physiology department. They measured electrical activity in the muscles of two groups of women (an accepted method of gauging relaxation). One group exercised for 20 minutes at 40 percent intensity; the other for 20 minutes at 75 to 80 percent.

Photograph 1-3. Grim? A hard ride can put the song back in your spirit.

The researchers found the muscles were about twice as relaxed after the higher intensity workout.

Interestingly, the same effect occurs whether a woman is naturally high-strung or laid-back. Dr. Bulbulian and Ebert compared this "tranquilizing effect" of exercise in type A and type B women. Type A personalities, according to Bulbulian, are "easily irritated, quick to lose their temper, and are driven by things like money and success." Type B personalities are "more easygoing, and view their jobs and their lives with less pressure." Researchers found that strenuous exercise reduced muscular tension similarly in both types of women.

Another factor that controls stress is diet. At Auburn University, Robert Keith, Ph.D, and Kathy O'Keeffe, M.S., gave a mood profile test to three groups of female cyclists. One group's diet consisted of 13 percent complex carbohydrate; the second group, 54 percent carbohydrate; and the third group, 72 percent carbohydrate. After a week, the medium- and high-carb groups showed no emotional differences, but the low-carbohydrate group was more tense, angry, depressed, as well as less vigorous.

The bottom line? No matter how stressed you feel, a spirited ride can help. And if you're overly tense for no apparent reason, maybe it's something you ate – or something you didn't eat.

Myth 2: I shouldn't ride a bike if I'm pregnant. Jackie Plate of Brooklyn, New York, used to enjoy riding hilly centuries. But she's eight months pregnant now and no longer cycles. Instead she swims half a mile four times per week and walks for exercise.

"I stopped working out altogether during my first trimester," says Plate, an active woman who has been trying to have a child for seven years, with one miscarriage. "My doctor was strongly against doing anything strenuous in the first trimester, so I just walked a little. I don't know if my level of exercise hurt my ability to become pregnant, but I didn't want to take any chances this time."

But did she have to be so cautious? Is trying to maintain or improve your fitness during pregnancy a waste of time? Will it lead to problems in delivery? Is the fetus at risk if you exercise? According to several new studies, the answers are no, no, no, and no.

First, you *can* improve your fitness during pregnancy, according to Pat Kulpa, M.D., an obstetrician and gynecologist in Grand Rapids, Michigan. Dr. Kulpa divided 141 pregnant women of varying fitness levels into two groups. One group cycled or did a similar type of exercise for one hour, three times a week, at 85 percent intensity. The other group remained mostly sedentary. Test results showed that the women who exercised actually improved their cardiovascular fitness.

Second, cycling won't complicate delivery. In fact, it can make it *easier.* "Some information suggests that the ease of delivery is enhanced in active women," says Dennis Dolny, Ph.D. "Cycling improves the heart and lung function. And the leg strength gained from cycling helps in taking on the skeletal stress that occurs with pregnancy." Dr. Kulpa's study showed exercise had no effect on the length of the pregnancy, type of delivery, or incidence of complication.

Third, exercise *won't* harm the fetus. In Dr. Kulpa's study, there were no differences in fetal birth weight, respiratory effort, muscle tone, or reflexes when comparing the active and sedentary women. Nor was there an increased risk of newborn death.

In another study, Dr. Dolny and Jennifer Beller, M.S., of the University of Idaho's Human Performance Laboratory, examined the effects of aerobic endurance exercise on maternal and fetal heart rate during the second and third trimester. They compared a group of sedentary expectant mothers with eight pregnant women who exercised for 20 minutes a day, three times a week, routinely raising their heart rate to 130 to 150 beats per minute (bpm). They also compared the heart rates of the fetuses, one of the most important indicators of a baby's well-being. Dr. Dolny and Beller found no evidence of fetal heart rate decline with exercise.

"There is no real cutoff point where a woman cyclist has to stop riding," concludes Dr. Dolny. "As the pregnancy progresses, it's more a matter of changing the duration and intensity of the workouts, keeping them in the range of activity that's proven safe to fetal heart rates." For instance, if you're accustomed to strenuous rides that raise your heart rate past 150 bpm, Dolny suggests slowing down and keeping it in the 140 to 150 bpm range.

Indeed, cycling is an excellent way to maintain cardiovascular fitness during pregnancy. Dr. Dolny says the upright riding posture is better for expectant mothers than more horizontal exercises that restrict blood flow. If the dangers of the road intimidate you, try a stationary bike.

Another advantage to cycling is that, like swimming, it's a non-weight-bearing activity. "It takes strain off joints," notes Dolny. "Once you get to the point in your pregnancy where sitting on the bike is too tough, swimming is an excellent alternative."

After the delivery, cycling and swimming are still a woman's best choices for activity. "Avoid jarring or pounding exercise," says Dr. Dolny, "especially if you've undergone any surgical procedure with your delivery."

Myth 3: Diet doesn't make a difference in my cycling performance. Adrien Rothschild, 38, of Baltimore, Maryland, has been cycling since 1968. For the last 16 years, she's also been a vegetarian. She knows the connection between good nutrition and performance.

"Being a vegetarian, I began to notice that I rode a lot better when I loaded up on carbohydrates such as rice and beans," says Rothschild.

If you want to realize your cycling potential, your diet should consist of at least 50 percent carbohydrate, according to Auburn University researchers who correlated nutrition and endurance performance of female cyclists.

As part of the same study that measured diet's effect on mood (see Myth 1), researchers Keith and O'Keeffe had women ride at 80 percent intensity until they fatigued and were unable to continue. They found that "exercise time for women on the low-carbohydrate diet was almost half that of women on the moderate-level diet." In other words, consuming a moderate amount of carbohydrate (about 50 percent of total diet) nearly doubles endurance. A high amount of carbo (72 percent of total diet) increases endurance even more.

"The reason is your body requires less oxygen to burn carbohydrate than fat," explains Dr. Wells of Arizona State University. "Carbohydrates are the most efficient kind of energy."

"When I first started riding," recounts Sherri Sharpe, a fast-recreational cyclist from Macon, Georgia, "it took me 1 hour to do 10 miles. I didn't think diet had anything to do with it. . . . Now probably 60 percent of my diet is carbohydrate and I have a lot more energy."

Myth 4: Calcium is the only preventive against osteoporosis. Osteoporosis is the loss of bone density due to a decrease in the female hormone estrogen. After a woman reaches menopause, her body doesn't produce as much estrogen. This can lead to bone deterioration, which manifests itself in low back pain, loss of physical stature, and frequent fractures.

Doctors and countless advertisements have recommended calcium-rich foods to help younger women ward off the problem. In addition, researchers say weight-bearing sports such as running, walking, and weightlifting help stimulate bone formation, keeping the problems associated with osteoporosis at bay. But does cycling provide the same benefits?

Yes – at least somewhat. The pedaling motion involves the contraction of muscles that attach to bone. "This contraction exerts a mechanical stress and improves bone formation," says Barbara Drinkwater, Ph.D., a Seattle research physiologist and president of the American College of Sports Medicine. "However, cycling alone may not be the best way to promote good bone formation through exercise."

Dr. Drinkwater recommends that women supplement their riding with running or walking. Dr. Wells adds that while "running and walking are good, they don't do anything for the upper body." She suggests a moderate weightlifting program that works the entire skeletal structure.

Dietarily, Dr. Wells says there's nothing wrong with taking calcium supplements, although "the jury is still out on how much good they do. The best way to get calcium is through natural sources such as dairy products."

Myth 5: There's nothing I can do about amenorrhea and premenstrual syndrome. Have you ever dramatically increased your training mileage and then started missing periods? If so, you've experienced athletic amenorrhea.

Temporary amenorrhea – as long as six months without a period – generally won't harm the reproductive system, although your gynecologist should be consulted. Longer amenorrheic spells can have serious implications. A related problem is that amenorrhea of any duration results in less estrogen in the bloodstream. Thus, later in life, a woman prone to amenorrhea might be more susceptible to osteoporosis.

Women with a low percentage of body fat often suffer amenorrhea. But a low level of body fat is not the sole cause. In fact, there is no conclusive evidence as to why amenorrhea occurs in athletes. According to Dr. Wells, there seem to be five key factors:

1. Intensity of training. Abrupt increases in intensity may contribute to the onset of amenorrhea. To avoid the risk, increase mileage and intensity gradually, i.e., 10 percent a week.

2. Type of activity. Different sports trigger different responses in a woman. A triathlete, for instance, might be able to ride 200 miles a week with no problem, but may start missing periods after adding 20 miles of running to her weekly routine. Monitor your training to determine the activity that might be causing the problem.

3. Stress. The pressures of training, competition, and everyday life can impinge on normal menstruation. The warning signs of stress include sudden changes in appetite, weight, recovery time after training, and resting pulse rate. If you notice any of these, slow down and relax.

4. Percentage of body fat. While there's no universally accepted range for ideal body fat percentage, sudden or large fluctuations in it or body weight can lead to amenorrhea.

5. Diet. Some women cyclists don't eat properly. According to Dr. Wells, new research shows that many competitive women athletes are severely underfed. "For example, many serious women athletes don't get the essential 12 to 15 percent of quality protein they need," she explains. "Or they simply don't eat enough."

The effect of diet on amenorrhea was underscored in a recent study by Dr. Drinkwater and Barbara Bruemmer, R.D. They found that women who eat red meat are less likely to miss periods. In fact, nearly half of the normally menstruating women in their study regularly ate red meat, while only 14 percent of the amenorrehic women did.

In general, balance and consistency seem to be the keys to avoiding amenorrhea. "If an athlete considers her training schedule, mental state, and diet," Dr. Wells explains, "and works out a program where all three are in balance, she greatly reduces any chance of amenorrhea."

Conversely, if the three are out of balance, Dr. Wells says you're "in a state of energy drain, and thus prone to the symptoms of imbalance, like amenorrhea and osteoporosis."

Sherri Sharpe, 28, averages more than 100 miles a week during her peak riding season and this is precisely the time she stops menstruating. When her training decreases, her periods return. Sharpe notices an opposite swing in the incidence of premenstrual syndrome (PMS). When she isn't riding as much, the PMS is slightly worse.

What Sharpe has learned through self-evaluation, researchers at the Human Performance Laboratory at Ball State University in Muncie, Indiana, have demonstrated in controlled tests. Their study compared PMS sufferers who exercised regularly with ones who were largely sedentary. They found that "the training group had a significant decrease in the average number of PMS symptoms," leading them to conclude that women can "reduce the number of PMS symptoms through the performance of regular physical activity" such as cycling.

Part Two
Get Started Right

Bicycles for Women

Women are built differently than men – but not the way you think. The typical woman has shorter arms and torso but longer legs than a man of the same height. She has narrower shoulders, smaller hands and feet, a wider pelvis, and less strength.

Because of these differences, her bike should be designed differently. The big difference: A woman's bike should have a shorter reach (stem length plus top tube length) than the typical man's bike.

But this is only half the picture. While the average male between 25 and 34 years old is 68 inches tall, his female counterpart, at 5 feet 4 inches, is 4 inches shorter. Thanks to legs that are longer in relation to overall height, however, the average woman can probably straddle a 19-inch diamond frame, the smallest size widely available. Until recently, anyone smaller had to settle for a step-through mixte or "lady's" frame, which is less rigid than the more desirable diamond or "man's" frame.

Problem is, mixtes may be designed for women but darn few 17- or 18-inch mixtes are *short* enough between seat tube and head tube. Most mixtes aren't proportioned correctly for the short-torsoed woman cyclist.

It's obvious that most bike manufacturers don't understand these basic differences between men and women. It's common on club rides to see women bravely pedaling two-wheeled torture racks with outstretched arms and locked elbows. And for each one you see on the road there are probably at least as many sitting home, unable to comprehend how anyone can enjoy an experience as painful as cycling.

Innovations in bicycle design tend to originate with custom builders. They're adopted by manufacturers only when educated consumers demand them. That's exactly what's happened with properly proportioned women's bikes. With women riders the fastest growing segment of the market and more women than men riding bikes, the big companies are rushing to introduce smaller models.

A few years ago, the 19-inch diamond frame was the smallest available with full-size wheels. Today, 17-inch (and smaller) models are vying for bike shop space. What's more, anatomic saddles that fit women, shorter crankarms, narrower handlebars, and down-sized brake levers and toe clips are standard equipment on these bikes. This pleases dealers who previously found themselves retrofitting these parts in order to clinch sales to women.

Road Bikes

When a woman is approximately 5 feet 4 inches or shorter, the fit requirements of her body proportions are more complicated. Two schools of thought have evolved on how to design road bikes for women that really fit.

The more creative solution starts with a frame geometry that provides handling characteristics identical to larger bikes and puts the person in a picture-perfect riding position. The result is an unusual-looking bike with mismatched wheels – a standard 700C or 27-inch rear wheel, and a smaller (usually 24-inch) front wheel. This is often referred to as a Terry-type bike in deference to framebuilder Georgena Terry, whose aggressive marketing popularized the design. Several major manufacturers have followed her lead and are producing bikes with small front wheels.

Terry's design shortens the top tube for a comfortable reach, but the toe clips do not strike the front wheel when it's turned. From a performance standpoint, a small wheel creates less wind resistance, especially if it has fewer spokes. It also allows you to get closer to another rider for a better draft. A smaller front tire has a slightly higher rolling resistance than a larger one, but this is more than offset by the aerodynamic advantage.

The small front wheel looks odd from the rider's perspective, but the fact that the frame has normal geometry means that it handles as well as a conventional bike. Weight distribution isn't seriously affected, but the illusion of sitting too far forward takes getting used to for some riders. Disadvantages of the design include the fact that if the bike is a bit small, too much of the rider's weight will be on the front wheel, adversely affecting cornering control.

In a race, the smaller wheel may also complicate a wheel change. The availability of 24-inch tires has improved, but selection is still limited compared to 700C clinchers and tubulars. The belief that mismatched wheel sizes requires carrying two spare tubes is incorrect, however. A full-size tube can be tucked into itself to fit a smaller tire.

Small bikes can also be designed with two standard-size wheels, although not without compromises. These bikes look more normal, allow wheels to be interchanged with those of larger bikes, and tires are widely available. Bike fit and handling depend on frame design and the rider's body dimensions. Usually, however, a 17½-inch or smaller frame that's designed for two 700C wheels has a geometry that increases high-speed stability at the expense of maneuverability. Even so, most bikes this small handle well as a result of the female rider's relatively light weight and low center of gravity.

Mountain Bikes

Unencumbered by "correct" looks and lacking the precise fitting systems of road bicycles, mountain bikes for small riders are consequently more varied in design. Some manufacturers use 24-inch front and rear wheels instead of the standard 26-inch, allowing a decent fit for riders as short as 4 feet 9 inches.

Larger wheels have advantages, however, including improved flotation over obstacles and greater tire availability. Thus, some mountain bike makers slope the top tube and make the frame as short as possible between two 26-inch wheels. A third approach is to mix wheel diameters for a Terry-type mountain bike.

Components

A good design for a small woman doesn't end with the frame and wheels. Most manufacturers recognize this when specing small bikes. For example, small hands need small brake levers, narrow shoulders require a narrow handlebar, short legs spin more efficiently with short crankarms, and petite feet need small toe clips. In addition, women generally prefer wide saddles with short noses. The result – *if* the designer is sensitive to the needs of the petite woman cyclist – is a downsized bike that's as comfortable, predictable, affordable, and fast as the same model in a larger size.

The Proper Fit

A bicycle's saddle and handlebar are adjustable, but its frame has fixed dimensions. If the tube lengths aren't carefully matched to your body proportions, you won't achieve a comfortable riding position.

To determine if your present bike or the one you're considering buying is the proper size, try this quick check: Wearing riding shoes, straddle the bike and measure the distance between your crotch and the top tube. If it's between 1 and 2 inches, you're on the money. If it's outside this range and you find it impossible to make some of the following adjustments, you need a different size bike. (Note: This doesn't apply to mountain bikes, which should be about 2 to 3 inches smaller than a properly sized road bike.)

But if it does basically fit, a run-through of the following procedures in the order discussed will give you a *well*-fitted bicycle.

Foot Position

Perfect riding position starts with the feet – the points through which energy is transferred to the bicycle. Improper foot position makes you a less efficient pedaler and overstresses the knees.

Contrary to the belief of many beginners, pedals aren't supposed to nestle in the arch of the foot: They belong under the ball of the foot. This permits the agility needed to spin and brings the calf muscles into play. Most recreational cyclists should position the ball of each foot directly over the pedal axle.

If you ride without toe clips it will be difficult to keep your feet properly positioned. Identify the center of the balls of your feet by making a mark on the outside of each shoe, then glance down occasionally to make sure the marks are in line with the pedal axle.

Toe clips are recommended because they help maintain proper foot position and increase pedaling efficiency. When the ball of your foot is over the pedal axle, the toe of your shoe should be about ⅛-inch from the end of the clip. This space is necessary to prevent pressure on your toes and damage to the ends of your shoes. If your foot size is between clip sizes, you can either use the larger size and have extra room, or select the smaller size and place washers between the pedals and clips to gain the needed extra space.

If you wear cleated cycling shoes, foot-over-pedal position becomes a function of cleat location. To find the balls of your feet through rigid-sole cycling shoes, Bill Farrell, developer of the Fit Kit sizing system, recommends painting a white dot on the ball of your right foot, then carefully pressing the foot to the sole of the left shoe (cleat removed) to transfer the paint. Do the same with the left foot and the right shoe and then drill a small hole though the dot on each sole. Attach the cleats so when the shoes are engaged with the pedals, the sole holes are over the center of the pedal axles.

Rotational adjustment of the cleats – the line they take in relationship to the rest of your foot – is critical, too. An unnatural foot position during pedaling will strain the knee. Simply positioning the feet straight ahead will work for some riders, but it's best to ride a few miles with the cleats loose enough to let your feet find their natural alignment. It's not uncommon for them to be at different angles. Have a friend reach underneath and tighten the cleats before you dismount. (If knee problems develop despite attempts to correctly adjust your cleats and overall riding position, visit a bike shop that uses the Fit Kit and its Rotational Adjustment Device, a cleat positioning tool.)

Saddle Tilt

Make sure the top of the saddle is level (or nearly so) with the ground. Lay a yardstick lengthwise on top and look at the angle between frame and top tube. Tilt the saddle *slightly* up or down only if doing so is necessary for comfort. Generally, it's risky to point the nose down because it can cause arm fatigue as you resist the tendency to slide forward.

Ride with very light pressure on the handlebar. If you slide forward, tilt the nose of the saddle up slightly. Go easy, because a high nose can cause crotch discomfort and numbness when you lean into the handlebar. Also, too much upward tilt will make you slide off the rear when you push hard on climbs.

Photograph 2-1. The top of your saddle should be level with the ground.

Saddle Height

The effort it takes to ride a bike is profoundly influenced by saddle height. Studies have shown that pedaling efficiency decreases rapidly when the saddle is located outside a particular rider's optimum range.

Efficiency isn't the same as power, however. Although the human leg can exert the most force when almost straight, pedaling a bicycle with the seat raised to such a height is unstable, inefficient, and can promote knee trouble. A saddle that's too low squanders efficiency and power. It prevents full use of the thigh muscles, yielding a poor return for the energy expended.

Photograph 2-2. If your stem is properly extended, a line dropped from the tip of your nose should cross it about 1 inch behind the handlebar.

Saddle height is directly related to inseam length – the longer the leg, the higher the saddle. Although every coach and framebuilder has a pet formula, one of the oldest still works well for the majority of riders. With your bare feet 6 inches apart, hold a tape measure firmly into your crotch and measure to the floor. (Have a friend help so you're exact.) Multiply this number by 1.09, then use the result to set the distance from the top of the saddle to the center of the pedal axle when the crankarm is parallel with the seat tube.

This method should put you within a centimeter of the ideal, with your knees slightly bent at the bottom of each pedal stroke. As you ride, make the necessary refinements.

Reach to Handlebar

The dimension that most affects upper body position is reach, the combined measurement of the top tube and handlebar stem extension. To determine if yours is correct, begin by putting the top of the handlebar 1 inch lower than the top of the saddle. This height should be fine for most riders. But never position the stem above its minimum insertion mark.

Next check for proper stem extension. Get on the bike and assume a normal riding position with hands on the bar drops and elbows slightly bent. Have a friend hold a plumb line (a nut on a string will do) to the end of your nose. It should fall about 1 inch behind the handlebar. If the plumb line misses the mark by much, you can estimate what size replacement stem you need.

Give It Time

After you've carefully made all these adjustments, *minor* aches and pains may develop before your body adapts to its new riding posture. This discomfort is normal, so resist the temptation to fiddle with your position. You'll become accustomed to it after a few rides, and your cycling performance will improve. At that point, you can start concentrating on bike-handling skills and fitness, confident that your riding position is as good as can be.

Fit Tips for Small Riders

If you're a small cyclist with a properly sized bike, here are some recommendations for equipment that will enhance riding comfort and efficiency even more.

Handlebar bars. For petite riders, the bars should be downsized. Among Japanese companies, SR offers drop bars as narrow as 36 centimeters measured the usual way, center to center. The smallest European bars that are widely available measure 38 centimeters. The Italian firm 3TTT advertises a 36-centimeter bar, but the company measures to the inside edges, making its 36 equal to everyone else's 38.

Handlebar stem. Steel handlebar stems as short as 3.5 centimeters are found on some English 3-speed bikes. Although not especially stylish, they offer almost 1 inch less reach than the shortest alloy stem. Attractive 6-centimeter stems are made by Specialized, SR, and 3TTT. To our knowledge, only SR offers a 5-centimeter alloy stem. Ask at your bike shop for part SR-50AH. Since not all stems fit all brands of handlebars, check with your shop about the feasibility of your intended combination.

Saddle. Women's anatomic saddles, made wider and shorter than conventional seats, are preferred by many female cyclists. Even so, some women racers prefer a well-padded standard design such as the Selle Italia Turbo. Test ride a few models to find what offers the best support for *your* anatomy.

Crankarms. Cranks shorter than the standard 170 millimeters are available through most bike shops. For cranks as short as 150 millimeters, you have only two choices: T.A. of France and Zeus of Spain. Replacing cranks isn't cheap, but a careful shopper can often locate a complete crankset in a local shop that costs less than special ordering a pair of short arms for existing chainrings.

Toe clips. There's no universal standard for toe clip sizes. Generally, Japanese clips run smaller than European brands, so a Japanese medium is about the same as an Italian or French small. Clips that are slightly too short can be moved forward by putting washers between the clip and pedal.

Brake levers. Just as small feet need small toe clips, small hands require downsized brake levers. Weinmann and Dia-Compe offer "junior" levers, and Shimano's Dura-Ace AX and 600 AX permit the reach to be adjusted.

To modify standard brake levers for smaller hands, try bending the handles toward the bar, or place a conical faucet washer between the top of the handle and the lever body, with the brake cable through the washer to hold it in place. Be aware that either method reduces the distance the lever can travel before it contacts the handlebar, so the brake pads must be kept adjusted close to the rim.

Learning the Lingo

Cycling has an entire language of its own. When a friend says she's planning a roller workout, don't expect to see curlers. When you're offered a pull, don't ask where to attach the towline. When you're called a wheelsucker, don't . . . well, you get the idea. To help avoid embarrassing situations, here's a page from the bikie's dictionary:

attack – to accelerate suddenly, pulling away from other riders
blocking – legally impeding the progress of riders in the pack to allow teammates in the break a better chance to stay away
bonk – when you completely run out of energy, or as marathoners say, hit the wall; occurs when glycogen stores are exhausted
break or breakaway – one or more cyclists who leave the main group of riders behind by going "off the front"
cadence – your rate of pedaling measured in revolutions per minute (rpm) for 1 foot
CAT I, II, III, IV – racing categories designated by the U.S. Cycling Federation (USCF), based on a rider's ability and/or experience, with Is having the most and IVs the least
century – a 100-mile ride
circuit race – a multilap road race on a course 2 miles or more in length
clincher – a tire with a detachable inner tube
criterium – a multilap event on a course 1 mile or less in length
domestique – a rider who sacrifices individual performance to work for the team leaders
dropped – failing to keep pace with the group of riders

drops – the part of the handlebar below the brake levers; also called hooks

echelon – a type of paceline in which riders angle themselves across the road in order to get the maximum draft in a crosswind

field sprint – a sprint to the finish by the main group of riders

fred – derisive term used by cycling snobs to describe novice riders or tourists

full tuck – an extremely crouched riding position used for fast descents

general classification – a rider's overall standing in a stage race; also called g.c.

gorp – a high-carbohydrate snack made from nuts, seeds, raisins, granola, candy, etc; stands for good old raisins and peanuts

hammering – riding as hard as possible; also known as jamming

hanging in – barely maintaining contact at the back of the pack

honking – standing with your hands on the brake lever hoods while climbing

hook – to deliberately move your back wheel into the front wheel of a pursuing rider

jump – a quick, hard acceleration

leadout – a race tactic in which a rider accelerates to maximum speed so a teammate can draft and then sprint past to the finish

metric century – a 100-kilometer (62-mile) ride

minuteman – in a time trial (TT), the rider who immediately precedes you in the starting order; so called because in most TTs riders start at 1-minute intervals

motorpacing – riding in the draft of a motorcycle or car to train in a big gear at 25 to 35 mph

off the back – describes one or more riders who have failed to keep pace with the main group

overgear – using a gear too big for the terrain or your level of fitness

paceline – a single-file, group formation in which each rider takes a turn breaking the wind at the front before pulling aside, dropping to the rear position, and recovering in the draft until reaching the front again

peloton – a large cluster of riders; also called pack, field, bunch

pizza elbow – see road rash

pull – to take a turn leading a group of riders; also referred to as pulling through

prime – (pronounced "preem") a prize or time bonus awarded to the winner of selected laps during a criterium or a track race; may also be given to the first rider reaching a certain point in a road race

pusher – a rider who pedals a big gear with a relatively slow cadence

road rash – any skin abrasion resulting from a fall

rollers – an indoor training device for bicycles that works somewhat like a treadmill

saddle time – time spent cycling

sag wagon – a motor vehicle that follows a group of riders, carrying equipment and lending assistance in the event of difficulty; sometimes called a broom wagon

sew-up – a tire with an encased inner tube; also called a tubular

sit on a wheel – to ride directly behind someone in order to benefit from the other rider's slipstream; also known as sitting in or wheelsucking

slingshot – to sprint around a rider after taking advantage of her slipstream

snap – the ability to accelerate quickly

soft-pedal – to rotate the pedals without actually applying power

spin – to pedal at high cadence

spinner – a rider who pedals in a moderate-to-small gear at a relatively fast cadence

squirrel – a nervous or unstable rider

stage race – a multi-day event that consists of point-to-point and circuit road races, time trials, and sometimes criteriums; the winner is the rider with the lowest elapsed time for all stages

stayer – a rider with the ability to pedal at a relatively high speed for long periods; also called a pacer

take a flyer – to suddenly sprint away from the group

tempo – fast riding at a brisk cadence

throw the bike – a racing technique in which a rider pushes the bike ahead of his body at the finish, hoping to edge another sprinting rider

time trial – a race against the clock over a set distance

tops – the section of handlebar between the stem and brake levers

track bike – a bike with no braking or shifting mechanisms

turkey – an unskilled cyclist

unship the chain – remove the chain
wheelsucker – someone who rides behind others and doesn't take a pull
wind up – steady acceleration to an all-out effort

Weekly Bike Maintenance

To keep your bike working efficiently and reliably, devote some time each week to cleaning, lubricating, and adjusting. Such general maintenance will also help you find a problem before it results in a breakdown.

Clean and Inspect

Put your bike in a workstand or against a support. Unless the frame is filthy, use a soft rag to polish it with a cleaner/wax such as Bike Elixir. If it *is* filthy, wash it with a brush and mild detergent, then rinse and dry thoroughly.

As you clean, inspect for frame damage. Look for bulges and cracks in the metal, especially at tube intersections. If you find any, have the problem evaluated by a pro mechanic. Use touch-up paint on scratches or chips that expose bare metal.

Next, dip a corner of your rag in a solvent such as kerosene, or spray it with a lubricant such as WD-40 or Tri-Flow. Wipe each component clean, inspecting for cracks, loose bolts, etc., as you work. Save the drivetrain (crankset and derailleurs) for last because they're usually the dirtiest.

Do not clean rims with solvent. This will leave an oily film that renders the brakes useless. Instead, wipe the rims with a clean, dry rag. Inspect each spoke hole for cracks and for ferrules pulling through. Look for dents or gouges in the sidewalls. Replace a damaged rim immediately.

Wipe the spokes and squeeze each pair to find any that are loose or broken. Spin each wheel and watch the rim where it passes the brake pads. If you see large wobbles or hops, have the wheel trued before riding again or the rim could become damaged beyond repair. Check for loose hub bearings by wiggling the rim side to side. There should be no play.

Examine each tire's tread for embedded glass or other debris. Potential puncture producers can often be removed before they work through the tire casing. Also check the tread and sidewalls for cuts and bulges. Damaged tires *must* be replaced immediately. Their failure is inevitable.

Squeezes and Wiggles

Firmly squeeze each brake lever. Anything pop loose? Make sure each pad contacts the rim properly and recedes about 2 millimeters when the lever is released. Make fine cable adjustments with the barrels on the calipers or brake levers.

Check the headset adjustment by squeezing the front brake lever and rocking the bike back and forth. Clunking indicates looseness. If it's okay, lift the front wheel slightly and nudge the handlebar. Does the headset seem to catch when the wheel points straight ahead? A worn or tight headset reduces steering control, so have it repaired soon. Place an ear against the tip of the saddle and turn the handlebar. Rumbling means the bearings are dry or dirty.

Grasp a crankarm and wiggle it side to side. There shouldn't be play. A loose crankset will impair shifting and wear out prematurely. Tap each chainring bolt. If one is loose, you'll hear it. Once a month, remove the pedals, unship (remove) the chain, and check the condition of the bottom bracket bearings by putting your ear to the saddle as you turn the crank.

While the pedals are off, turn their axles and feel for roughness. Inspect the toe clips for cracks and loose bolts. Check the straps for wear and damaged buckles.

Grasp the saddle by the tip and tail, and shake it in all directions. Do the same with the handlebar. Tighten anything that slips. Check the nuts and bolts on accessories such as bottle cages and racks. Make sure there's a fresh spare tube or tire in your tool kit, and be certain your frame pump works.

Lube and Inflate

Two sure and simple ways to help your bike work well are to maintain proper tire pressure and to frequently lubricate your chain. Full tires roll efficiently and protect your rims from damage. A lubed chain shifts better, runs quieter, and lasts longer.

Chain maintenance is a simple matter of wiping the links clean with a rag, then applying a lubricant. This can be done with the chain on the bike. If the chain is covered with sludge, however, you'll need to remove it and use a solvent.

Recommended tire pressure is usually printed on the sidewall. In general, high-pressure clinchers and training tubulars require about 110 psi. If you're in doubt, call a bike shop. Most floor pumps with a built-in gauge are reasonably accurate. The pumps at gas stations are risky to use because they quickly deliver a large volume of air, which can blow out a bike tire.

Once you've established your weekly maintenance routine, the work will take only about 20 minutes. This small amount of time pays off big in confidence, safety, and smooth, efficient riding.

Part Three
Training and Nutrition

"The Best Riding Tips I Know"

Connie Carpenter Phinney won a gold medal in the women's road race at the 1984 Olympics. Mark Gorski did the same in the match sprint. Together they represent a wealth of experience and success. We asked each of them for their top riding tips. What follows are 18 ways to make yourself a better cyclist. And while they might not put you on the podium at the next Olympics, they *will* help you excel at the sport and enjoy it more.

1. See Success

Mark: By envisioning yourself excelling on the bike, whether it be in a time trial or a century, you'll boost your self-confidence and, many times, turn the dream into reality. I imagined winning the Olympic gold medal so many times I felt as if I was supposed to win – like I was "experienced" in the situation.

Visualization is a simple technique that anyone can benefit from. All that's needed is a comfortable, quiet place. Relax for a few minutes, close your eyes, and imagine yourself in the situation you want to excel in. Picture everything about the situation – the course, the scenery, the competition. *Feel* the atmosphere, the weather, the excitement, and your own apprehension. Then imagine yourself realizing your goal. *Feel* the satisfaction and the joy of achievement. Do this a few times a day and you'll become a more successful, highly motivated rider.

2. Weight Your Outside Leg on Descents

Connie: Descending is one of the most difficult aspects of bicycle racing. At the world-class level, races are often won or lost on daring downhill moves. In my first year of racing I struggled desperately with the descent on the world championship road race course in Italy. My performance was so poor in training that the coaches kept toting me back to the top to practice. I was told to follow veteran Miji Reoch through the tricky hairpins. It paid off, as I was one of the first riders at the bottom of the hill on race day.

When cornering during a descent, it's natural to pull your inside leg up (i.e., right turn, right leg up; left turn, left leg up), but few riders think to weight the extended, outside leg. This is a fundamental skill of downhill skiing. By weighting the leg, I mean putting pressure on the outside pedal. This can be taken one step further by weighting the outside arm and gripping the handlebar a bit tighter with the outside hand. In all, it increases your stability and enables you to negotiate descents safely and quickly.

3. Stretch Regularly

Mark: Stretching is important for several reasons. For one, it's the best prevention against injuries. Second, stretching improves performance. If you're not flexible, your body recruits less-efficient muscles and wastes energy. Stretching should be done every day. In fact, frequency is the most important factor in any stretching program. Each stretch should be held for a minimum of 15 to 20 seconds. There should be no bouncing. Incorporate a variety of stretches in your daily program including stretches for the neck, upper body, lower back, and legs. I recommend neck rolls, arm swings, trunk twisters, side bends, toe touches from the standing and seated position, calf stretches, knee-to-chest holds, sprinter's and hurdles stretches, and the human pretzel.

4. Relax

Connie: Many cyclists are needlessly tense on the bike. The combination of perceived road danger (traffic, potholes, etc.)

and inner stress ("I only have an hour to ride") can make cycling unenjoyable. Look for such warning signs as a death grip on the handlebar, locked elbows, stiff shoulders, and tight calves.

Make yourself relax. Grip the bar lightly, or with "butterfly fingers" as my gymnastics instructor used to say. Flutter your fingers (one hand at a time) and consciously relax each one. Then bend your elbows and drop your shoulders. Take a deep breath. Tension in the arms often forces the shoulders together, so make sure they stay relaxed. Tightness in the calves may make you pedal with toes pointed. To fix this, drop your heels to encourage a full pedal stroke. One other tip: To help relax on the bike, try stretching off the bike. I like to stretch after a ride to release tension and to stay loose until my next workout.

5. Learn to Spin

Mark: Learning to spin the pedals quickly and effectively is a technique that's overlooked by many riders. To be a successful cyclist you must have this ability. Simply put, maintaining a cadence of 85 to 90 revolutions per minute (rpm) is the most efficient way to propel a bicycle.

Start by working on your flexibility. Stretching for 10 minutes before a workout will prepare your muscles for high-rpm pedaling and dramatically improve your efficiency and smoothness on the bike. The other key to efficient spinning is just as simple – do it for many, many miles. Spend the first four to six weeks of each season spinning a 42×18 or smaller gear. You'll be doing well if you can ride comfortably at 18 mph for 20 miles.

6. Ride Slow

Connie: No great champion rides at the same speed all the time, but many recreational riders do. In order to learn to ride fast, you must first learn to ride slow. To do so, take a "bike walk" at least once a week. This is an easy 10- to 15-mile ride in a small gear, say a 42×21. The first time I did this was under national team coach Eddie Borysewicz in 1977. We would train hard in the morning, rest in the early afternoon, then go for a late afternoon bike walk. I still remember the fun we had.

Photograph 3-1. Trunk twisters.

Photograph 3-2. Side bends.

Photograph 3-3.
Knee-to-chest holds.

Photograph 3-4. Sprinter's stretch.

Photograph 3-5. Reverse hurdles stretch.

Photograph 3-6. Human pretzel.

The purpose of this type of training is to learn to relax on your bike. It's a great recovery tool, also: Explore new roads or ride with friends you generally consider too slow. Better yet, ride with your regular training partners and do some small-gear sprints. Before long, you'll feel more confident and in control on your regular training rides.

7. Do Quality Workouts

Mark: Lack of training time is a common problem among fast recreational riders. But it needn't keep you from realizing your potential. Maximize the time you spend on your bike by making each ride a quality workout. If you train during your lunch hour, stretch for 10 minutes beforehand to reduce your on-bike warm-up time. After 10 minutes of easy pedaling, hold an 85 to 90 percent effort for 10 minutes in a larger gear (52×17 or 52×16). Recover with a couple of minutes of easy, high-rpm pedaling, then do four 5-minute intervals at maximum effort, pedaling easily for 2 minutes in between. Cool down for 10 minutes in a small gear and your quality workout is complete.

8. Never Climb in the Drops

Connie: I often see riders so intent on getting to the top of a hill they hunch over the handlebar drops. This is the most inefficient position for climbing because it constricts breathing and thereby deprives your muscles of valuable oxygen. *Always sit up when climbing.* Put your hands on the brake lever hoods, hold your head high, and keep your shoulders wide.

9. Never Ride with Earphones

Connie: There is nothing more dangerous than riding with Walkman-type earphones. Doing so deprives you of one of your most crucial senses. My hearing is refined from years of riding. I can hear trucks coming from far away, and can even gauge how close they might come. On several occasions I've moved onto the shoulder because my ears told me the truck was too close for comfort.

10. Work on Bike Handling

Mark: In order to ride in a group, negotiate traffic, and avoid accidents, you must be adept at handling your bike. The way I developed the necessary confidence was by racing clunker bikes with friends. One of our favorite games involved marking an oval course in a grassy field. We wore old clothes and protective gear, and got physical. We bumped elbows, shoulders, knees, and tried to rub our front wheels against another rider's rear tire without crashing. A few sessions like this will improve your bike-handling ability dramatically. Plus, you'll have a lot of fun.

11. Dominant Hand = Rear Brake

Connie: Controlled braking is essential for safe riding, but one thing often overlooked by cyclists is brake position. If you're righthanded, your rear brake should be controlled by your right hand. If you're lefthanded, your rear brake should be controlled by your left hand. Why? Because the rear brake can be used with more force than the front one. Too heavy a hand on the rear brake may cause a skid, but a good rider will usually be able to check it. Too much force on the front brake, however, can catapult you over the handlebar. As a result, the front brake should only be used for fine-tuning.

At the 1983 World Championships I crashed because my brakes were switched to compensate for a broken arm. When I braked to avoid a skidding rider on a steep, rain-slickened road, I was reacting *against* my instincts. If I hadn't broken my arm and been forced to change my braking pattern, I wouldn't have crashed.

12. Lift Weights in Winter

Mark: Weight training will help you sprint faster, push bigger gears, and climb more powerfully and efficiently. For me, it meant the difference between being a decent international sprinter and Olympic champion.

There are several methods of weight training. Nautilus and Universal machines are easy to use and generally safe for beginners. Free weights require more expertise but allow for more varied workouts. The key to either: professional instruction. Have someone at a local health club show you the basics and – if possible – design a program that fits your personal schedule and goals.

In general, a good winter program consists of three sessions a week (every other day) with eight to ten exercises per workout equally divided between upper and lower body. Do three sets of 15 to 20 repetitions (reps) for each exercise. Rest a minute between each set. And always try to work with a weight that's difficult to lift on the last few reps.

During the riding season, you can hang on to most of your new upper body strength by doing one set of each exercise twice a week. Riding itself eliminates the need to do leg exercises.

13. Find Your Second Wind

Connie: You're riding hard and breathing heavy. Your legs are burning and you're about to be dropped. What can you do to save yourself?

First, concentrate on form. Most tired riders get sloppy, permitting excessive body and bike movement. Focus on your technique and watch for signs of tension (see tip 4, *Relax*). Since fatigue usually leads to rapid, shallow breathing, try inhaling forcefully. Think about your pedal strokes and try to rest on the stroke when you inhale. By taking control of the situation instead of letting it control you, you'll have a better chance of catching a "second wind": nothing more than your body's return to a steady-state condition, where the work being done is fueled by adequate oxygen and energy. Your body has tremendous potential, and with a little control you can expand its limits.

14. Dress Properly

Mark: If you're uncomfortable on the bike because you're not properly dressed, performance and overall enjoyment will suffer. Obviously, what you wear during summer is less critical than in spring, fall, and winter. When it's below 40 degrees, pay special attention to your head, feet, and hands. Wear a thin hat or earwarmers under your helmet. Shoecovers are a necessity as are ski gloves. Two pairs of tights might be needed along with several layers on your upper body. Use Chapstick or petroleum jelly on your lips to keep them from cracking.

Don't shed your tights until the temperature goes above 60 degrees. If your body has to struggle to stay warm, less blood will be available for working muscles. If there's any doubt, wear tights – you can always take them off. And sunglasses are a wise choice in any season: They protect your eyes from bugs and dirt while minimizing fatigue.

15. Diversify Your Training

Connie: It takes more than riding lots of miles to become a good cyclist. By diversifying your training you'll stimulate interest and improve overall body strength and endurance. The concept of cross-training popularized by triathletes isn't new. As a speedskater, I spent my summers cycling. Former world champions Beth Heiden, Sheila Young-Ochowicz, and Connie Paraskevin-

Young were also successful speedskaters before becoming cyclists. Other elite riders, such as world champion Jeannie Longo and '84 Olympic medalist Steve Hegg, came to cycling from downhill skiing.

If you live in a warm climate where it's possible to ride year-round, consider taking a month or two off from cycling to pursue other sports or develop a sound weight training program. I always loved the off-season because I had the luxury of a diverse training schedule. For those in cold climates, I can't think of anything worse than spending the winter on an indoor resistance trainer. Have fun in the off-season and take advantage of winter's unique opportunities. Ski and skate, or hike in deep snow. You might also supplement your early- and late-season cycling with weight training, swimming, and running.

16. Ride with a Group

Mark: Riding alone can be a peaceful, therapeutic experience. But cycling with a group also has its advantages. For one, it's good motivation. If you're committed to riding with friends, it's more difficult to skip a workout. Second, even disciplined athletes need to be pushed. Riding with a group usually results in a longer, harder workout. Plus, riding in a paceline helps you hone your bike-handling skills. But perhaps the best thing about riding with other people is the sheer *fun* that's involved: A ride that seems to drag forever when you're alone passes quickly with a group. Join a bike club and see if your performance and overall enjoyment of the sport don't improve.

17. Play

Connie: Plato said: "What, then, is the right way of living? Life must be lived as play." When your cycling becomes work, something is wrong. Play a little. Venture off-road on a mountain bike. Or take a leisurely weekend tour with your spouse. You'll renew your energy and enthusiasm if you ride for fun as well as fitness.

18. Set Goals

Mark: Setting goals is vital to the development of any cyclist. Many riders become frustrated when they don't see regular improvement in themselves. If you set realistic goals, however, you'll have a great motivational tool and a way of measuring improvement. A common mistake among riders is setting goals that are too lofty. Many people ask me if I always dreamed of winning a gold medal. The honest answer is that although I did dream about being in the Olympics, I never thought about winning the gold medal until about 1982. My goals as I came up through the ranks were always set one week or one month ahead, not ten years. This is the key for riders at all levels – set realistic, short-term goals. After a couple of years, you'll be able to look back and say, "Gee, I've really come a long way."

Five More Training Tips

1. Divide Each Calendar Year

This concept, called periodization, allows for maximum variety and improvement.

Off-season (October, November, December). Ride for enjoyment several times a week, but also run, hike, swim, ski, or do aerobics – anything that helps keep you fit. Lift weights to strengthen muscles that cycling neglects. The goal is variety and total body fitness.

Preseason (January, February, March). Increase time on the bike or indoor resistance trainer and reduce other sports. Weight train three times a week until March, then twice a week as you ride more.

Early season (April, May). Without neglecting endurance, train in ways that improve power and speed, such as hill climbs, intervals, time trials, fast club rides, and races. Weight train at least once a week to maintain your strength.

In-season (June, July, August, September). Do your thing. These are the months you have worked for since the previous autumn. Reduce training volume and increase quality. Count events as workouts, and include them in your overall plan so you don't overtrain. If you start feeling stale or fatigued, take several days off.

2. Build a Mileage Base

The general rule is to accumulate one-third of your esti-mated yearly mileage by doing steady aerobic work at a spinning cadence (90-plus pedal rpm) before advancing to hard climbing or big gears. If you don't condition muscles and tendons for the strain, injury may occur. Those who can ride consistently all winter may be able to retain a base from year to year, but if inclement weather or reduced daylight keeps you off the bike for several months, be patient in the spring and rebuild.

3. Monitor Your Progress

Keep a training diary. Each morning, record your pulse rate so you can spot an upward trend that signals overtraining. Also, weigh yourself to guard against dehydration and rapid weight loss, which leads to fatigue.

Detail the length of your rides in miles and minutes, the terrain, weather, gears used, and effort. Write how you felt, whether it was "Great!" or "Rotten." Then evaluate this informa-tion regularly to see what works and what doesn't. *Don't* make the common mistake of keeping a diary just to build an impres-sive mileage total. Within your written words is information as valuable as any coach can provide.

4. Get Enough Rest

You'll improve only if you rest enough to let your body adapt to the stresses of training. Take a day off once a week and go for a moderate spin on two or three other days. Three hard days a week is the maximum, and most fitness riders would do better with two.

5. Don't Overcoach Yourself

In cycling, careful attention to detail will make you better – to a point. You want to be dedicated, not obsessive. Work on your weaknesses, but never forget that the best reason for riding a bike is to have fun.

Meals for the Miles

When you reach into your jersey for a banana during a ride, that piece of fruit begins a journey more fascinating and magical than even the greatest bicycle tour. By the end of its trip, that banana – or sandwich, cookie, or whatever you ate – is transformed into energy, the key to completing *your* journey.

The Fuel of Choice

The process begins with a piece of food and the three main compounds it contains: carbohydrates, proteins, and fats.

"Your body breaks down the energy stored in the molecules of the food," says Edward Coyle, Ph.D., director of the Human Performance Laboratory at the University of Texas at Austin and a member of *Bicycling* magazine's Fitness Advisory Board.

"Carbohydrates are the preferred source of energy because your body can break them down faster than fat. Therefore, they rapidly release the energy needed for a vigorous ride."

Protein is rarely used for energy, although it does play other crucial roles in the body. Conversely, dietary fat is stored as an energy source, either in the blood as free fatty acids, in muscle fiber, or beneath the skin. You burn more body fat on long, slow rides, which is why such efforts are often recommended for

Photograph 3-7. Carbohydrates are a key component of any cyclist's diet.

losing weight. But this logic is flawed, at least according to Coyle. An hour of slow riding *will* burn fat. But when you eat later, the calories will only replenish those fat stores. A better weight-loss approach is to burn as many calories as you can by riding hard. In any case, fat is the body's secondary fuel source.

"When you're burning fat, you can't exercise at more than 50 to 60 percent of your aerobic capacity," says Dr. Coyle. "For instance, if you can normally maintain 24 mph, you won't be able to ride much faster than 15 mph for more than 5 to 10 minutes when you're burning fat. When you're on a fairly intense ride – maintaining a heart rate of 150 to 160 beats per minute – you only get about 40 percent of your energy from fat. The rest comes from carbohydrates. This is your body's fuel of choice."

How Carbohydrates Work

As they travel through your digestive system, carbohydrates – natural compounds coming from starches and sugars – are converted into glucose. The glucose is then transformed into its storage status, known as glycogen. Some glycogen goes to the liver where it's reconverted into glucose and dumped into the circulatory system. Meanwhile, other carbohydrates are stored in the muscles as muscle glycogen. This process, however, occurs at a much slower rate.

"Early in a ride, you rely almost exclusively upon muscle glycogen for energy," explains Dr. Coyle. "But as your muscle glycogen levels decline, you rely more on blood glucose. In just three hours of riding, the percentage of carbohydrate energy coming from muscle glycogen steadily declines from 100 percent to zero, while energy from blood glucose increases from zero to 100 percent."

After a few hours of pedaling without food, your glycogen and glucose stores will be depleted. Even if you have ample fat stores, the process through which these are converted to energy is not efficient enough to sustain the effort. With less fuel reaching your brain and muscles, you'll begin to feel dizzy and fatigued. Eventually, you'll run out of fuel – a condition cyclists call the bonk.

But what if you'd been ingesting carbo-rich foods and liquids during the ride? Could such feedings replenish your blood glucose stores fast enough to forestall the bonk?

"Five years ago, the scientific consensus was no – carbohydrate feedings don't contribute significant energy for exercise," says Dr. Coyle. "The thinking was that you shouldn't bother with so-called energy drinks because they couldn't be used rapidly enough by the body. But we're finding this isn't correct. The body can use carbohydrates during the latter stages of exercise when muscle glycogen is very low. We tested cyclists between the third and fourth hour of a ride and found they weren't using any muscle glycogen. *All* their carbohydrate energy was coming from the glucose they were drinking."

Dr. Coyle has shown that if cyclists eat and drink while riding, they can extend their endurance despite the fact that their muscle glycogen is exhausted. In a recent study he had two groups of cyclists ingest either a placebo or carbohydrates prior to bonking. Those who ingested the carbohydrates were able to cycle 45 to 60 minutes longer.

"Normally, you start to fatigue and the end comes quickly – You bonk and it's over," Dr. Coyle says. "But with steady carbohydrate feeding, you may fatigue but you're still able to grind it out."

Energy Drinks

Having demonstrated the effectiveness of carbohydrate feeding, Coyle is now working to dispel some other myths.

For instance, experts used to believe that an energy drink

Photograph 3-8. Energy drinks can help cyclists replace fluids and carbohydrates simultaneously.

should not contain more than 2.5 percent carbohydrate. It was thought that anything more would slow the solution's passage from stomach to intestines. This would have two negative effects. First, it would take longer for the body to absorb the fluid, inhibiting its ability to cool itself through sweating. Second, slow emptying of the stomach would cause nausea.

Dr. Coyle agrees that high concentrations of carbohydrates slow gastric emptying, but disagrees with the consequences.

"The stomach can empty a liter of water per hour, but it can only empty 800 milliliters per hour of a 5 percent carbohydrate solution," he notes. "Statistically this is significant, but functionally, it doesn't constitute a big difference. No one has been able to prove that the slowdown in gastric emptying makes any difference in the body's ability to cool itself."

In fact, some recent studies have shown the opposite. Research at Ball State University compared the gastric emptying effects of ingesting 5, 6, and 7 percent solutions during a long ride. All the solutions were readily emptied from the stomach and resulted in extended performance. Meanwhile, a University of South Carolina study compared 6 and 12 percent solutions. This one was conducted at 91-degree temperatures to gauge the effect on sweating. The 12 percent dose did not alter the body's ability to cool itself but it did cause some upset stomachs.

Nausea is the main reason extremely high concentrations still aren't universally accepted. When Dr. Coyle recently fed cyclists a 10 percent carbohydrate solution, 10 percent of the subjects vomited. "When you start ingesting solutions that have 7 to 10 percent or more carbohydrate, it can build up in the stomach and cause gastric distress," he explains. "But it's very individual. Some people can tolerate any concentration and empty it quickly. The key is to experiment and find what's best for you."

Dr. Coyle explains that during exercise the body can draw glucose from the blood at the rate of 1 gram per minute, or 60 grams per hour. Thus, to be effective, an energy drink should deliver between 40 and 60 grams of carbohydrate per hour. To accomplish this, you can drink either a little of a very concentrated solution, or a lot of a diluted solution. Doing the latter will also help you meet your fluid replacement needs. However, with a 2.5 percent solution you'd have to drink several liters per hour – difficult at best, impossible at worst.

Food for Fuel

Another bit of dated logic contends that eating carbo-rich foods immediately before a ride stimulates the secretion of insulin and causes fatigue. Insulin is a hormone that actually removes glucose from the blood. When combined with exercise, this can result in a dramatic drop in blood glucose, a condition called hypoglycemia. In susceptible individuals, the symptoms include cold sweat, headache, confusion, hallucinations, convulsions, and even coma. At the very least, the scarcity of glucose leads to lightheadedness and lower performance. But Dr. Coyle sees it differently.

"It's overrated. Most riders never sense it," he says. "We've found that fewer than 25 percent of those who experience hypoglycemia ever have a central nervous system effect where they feel shaky or irritable. Early in a ride, it's of almost no consequence. Only 1 in 30 people notice the effects. Later, they'll notice the depletion of blood glucose because they're depriving their muscles of energy. At this point, they may be able to tolerate the effects of hypoglycemia, but they can't tolerate the fact that their legs lack energy.

"By ingesting carbohydrate throughout the ride," Dr. Coyle continues, "you're providing the muscles with extra energy and thus you're able to ride longer."

But why can't you just keep ingesting carbohydrates and cycle indefinitely?

"Nobody knows," says Dr. Coyle. "We've studied cyclists riding with low levels of muscle glycogen but high levels of blood glucose. Their muscles seemed to be taking in glucose adequately. But after extending the exercise for about an hour, they had a second fatigue and they stopped. Something else is going on other than carbohydrates. We just don't know what."

A recent study at the University of Waterloo, Ontario, also concluded that other unknown factors besides carbohydrate availability cause fatigue.

Expert Advice

Even if science can't show you how to pedal indefinitely, you can improve your cycling performance and extend endurance significantly by using carbohydrates correctly – especially on glycogen-depleting rides of three hours or more. For instance:

A few days before a ride. Ingest 600 grams of carbohydrate per day, says Dr. Coyle. This will have your glycogen stores brimming.

A few hours before a ride. It's not as critical what you eat, says Dr. Coyle, as long as you've eaten well the previous few days and the night before.

During a ride. "On any ride longer than 3 hours," says Dr. Coyle, "bring bagels, an energy drink – anything high in carbohydrates. Liquids are easier to consume and provide necessary fluid. I suggest a carbohydrate concentration between 5 and 10 percent in volumes of 200 to 400 milliliters every 15 minutes. [A standard water bottle holds 590 milliliters.]"

Don't ignore solid food. "Carbohydrates are treated the same way by your body, regardless of whether they're liquid or solid," Dr. Coyle says. "In fact, it's good to mix solids with fluids, especially on long rides. I work with cycling teams and provide them with all types of carbohydrate fluid alternatives during races and hard rides. But once they've been riding about 6 hours, they all say the same thing: 'I want something solid.' "

Next time, hand them a banana, and let the real ride begin.

Different Rides, Different Diets

Different types of rides require different types of nutritional preparation. For example, if you eat for a century as you would for an interval workout, or vice versa, you'll be in trouble. Each type of ride has its own list of nutritional do's and don'ts. Here, sports nutritionist Liz Applegate, Ph.D., explains all the rules, including how, what, and when to eat for the five most common types of rides.

Commute

Steady speed, light to moderate effort. Distance: 5 to 20 miles. Time: less than 90 minutes.

In preparing nutritionally for a commute, you should have two goals: (1) to ride comfortably and (2) to have enough energy left to last the day.

For morning commutes, have a high-carbohydrate breakfast that includes fruit, cereal, skim milk, and whole-grain bread or muffins. For lunch or an afternoon snack, eat nutritional foods such as pasta, fruits, and vegetables.

However, never let commuting get in the way of maintaining a balanced diet. Do not, for example, purposely avoid foods rich in protein. This can lead to long-term performance problems and dangerously affect your health.

In general, allow yourself 30 to 45 minutes for digestion before you begin pedaling. And if you need a morning jolt to get going, remember that although the caffeine in coffee, tea, or cola might give you that "get-up-and-go" feeling, it's also a diuretic: Large amounts will cause your body to *lose* fluid and magnify the losses you'll incur while riding. This lowers performance. In fact, fluid replacement should be your primary concern during a commute. Drinking about one bottle of water per hour should be sufficient unless it's extremely hot and humid.

Middle Distance

Basic training ride, moderate intensity. Distance: 15 to 50 miles. Time: 45 minutes to 3 hours.

There are two nutritional dangers to avoid on training rides. The first is allowing your energy stores to become depleted, a condition known as bonking. This can happen on rides of 2 hours or more. The second is dehydration – a loss of body fluid that results in sluggishness.

You can avoid both conditions by using energy drinks. These mixtures supply carbohydrates and liquid simultaneously in a form that's quickly used by the body. Resist the temptation to rely exclusively on these drinks, however. Cyclists still need to drink water on long rides, since sweat loss outweighs the need for energy replacement. Carry two bottles – one filled with an energy drink and the other with plain water. Alternately drink from each one every 10 to 20 minutes.

About 20 minutes before a training ride, you should also

drink 8 to 20 ounces of water. This is particularly important during the summer, when you sweat more.

There are other key nutrition rules to remember. For instance, never eat fatty foods prior to riding. Pastries, chocolate, and cream cheese take longer to digest and contain less readily available fuel. In fact, carbohydrates should comprise 60 to 70 percent of your daily caloric intake, especially if you ride on consecutive days. Since individual needs are different, you may want to carry a high-carbo snack as well, such as the high-energy PowerBar used by 7-Eleven team riders. For a 2-hour ride, about 100 to 200 calories should be enough.

Intervals

Variable speed, high-intensity efforts interspersed with active recovery. Distance: 10 to 30 miles. Time: 30 minutes to 2 hours.

Interval training is the best way to become a faster cyclist. It's also a good way to drown your muscles with excess lactic acid. Intense exertion produces lactic acid within the muscles, which eventually inhibits their ability to contract. It's been theorized that certain foods, such as cranberries and prunes, work as a buffer against acid buildup and delay muscle fatigue. But there's still no evidence to support this. In fact, there's a much more important factor involved – blood. Blood is largely responsible for flushing away metabolites such as lactic acid during high-intensity workouts.

To make sure that blood *is* available when it's needed, you should allow 2 to 4 hours for digestion before an intense ride. You should also drink at least 16 ounces of water beforehand since perspiration losses will be great.

When riding, drink water between every interval. You don't need energy drinks or food snacks on this type of ride unless your total saddle time will exceed 2 hours. If it will, drink easily processed fluids such as diluted juices or an energy drink.

Hills

More than 50 percent of the route involves climbing. Distance: 10 to 30 miles. Time: 2½ hours or less.

A hilly ride taps your carbohydrate reserves. The key here is to plan ahead and eat a preride meal of about 600 calories – e.g., yogurt, bagel, fruit, low-fat cookies – 2 to 4 hours beforehand.

If you do this and still run low on fuel, experiment with foods and liquids that are high in sugar, such as soda, undiluted fruit juices, and cookies. Ingest them just before riding (15 minutes or less), and the sugar will usually kick in when your legs begin to fade.

Preride nutrition is especially important for a hilly outing because eating on the bike is virtually impossible. However, you can usually still get some energy replenishment during the ride. Just fill a water bottle with an energy drink, and take swigs whenever you're descending or the grade softens.

After the ride, refueling is essential to ensure proper recovery after such a hard effort. If you eat enough carbohydrate and drink plenty of fluid, your glycogen stores will be nearly back to normal in 24 hours. There are supplemental carbohydrate products (Gatorlode, Carboplex, Exceed) that are specifically designed to help you refuel properly without spending all night at the dinner table.

Long Distance

Steady speed, low to moderate intensity. Distance: 50 to 100 miles or more. Time: 4 hours plus.

A century is one type of ride on which you can't survive with bad nutrition. When a cyclist fails on a long ride, it's usually due to poor eating. The key is good planning before, during, and after the big event.

During a century, you'll probably ride slower than normal, which means you'll burn more fat for energy. Nonetheless, carbohydrate stores are still the limiting factor. Make sure yours are high by eating lots of carbo-rich foods in the days preceding the event. Take it easy on the bike the final day or two before the ride, and your muscles will be packed with glycogen.

Plan carefully for how and what you'll eat during the ride. Most organized centuries feature snack stops. If not, carry sandwiches made with moderately low-fat ingredients such as jam, honey, apple butter, and bananas, or other high-carbo snacks.

Nibble throughout the ride. Your body handles a steady intake of small food portions much better than one overload.

Forget high-fat goodies such as candy bars. These provide more fat and less carbohydrate than you need, as well as few necessary vitamins and minerals. Soda which contains caffeine may provide some energy (most likely due to its sugar content), but research shows that caffeine has less effect if you're a daily user.

TABLE 3-1.
Carbohydrate Calorie Counter

Fruit
Banana – 105
Pear – 98
Blueberries (1 cup) – 82
Apple – 81
Orange – 62
Raspberries (1 cup) – 61
Grapes (½ cup) – 57
Strawberries (1 cup) – 45

Cereal
Rice Chex (1⅛ cups) – 112
Cheerios (1¼ cups) – 111
Corn Chex (1 cup) – 111
Wheat Chex (⅔ cup) – 104
Shredded Wheat with fruit
    (⅔ cup) – 100

Bagel
Plain – 160 to 200

Low-Fat Cookies
Vanilla wafers (7) – 130
Animal crackers (15) – 120
Graham crackers (4) – 120
Ginger snaps (7) – 115

Fruit-Filled Cookies
Fruit bars, raisin-filled
    biscuits – 53 each

Sandwich
Pita bread filled with sliced
    fruit or shredded
    vegetables, plain or with a
    small amount of low-calorie
    dressing – 165

Dried Fruit (1¼ cups)
Figs – 127
Pears – 118
Raisins – 109
Peaches – 96
Prunes – 96
Apricots – 78
Apples – 52

Fruit Roll-Ups
1 roll (½ ounce) – 50

SOURCE: Diane Drabinsky, "Carbohydrate Calorie Counter," *Bicycling*, July 1988, p. 79.

Of course, fluid replacement is crucial. Carry at least four water bottles if there are no water stops along the route. For carbo nourishment, you can rely on either solid foods or energy drinks.

Remember that eating right doesn't stop when the ride ends. Within 6 hours after your long ride, it's important that you replenish exhausted glycogen stores. If you plan to ride again the next day, start eating and drinking immediately to ensure proper refueling.

A century is a great achievement and you may want to toast yourself with a glass of champagne at ride's end. But wait a few hours if you can. Alcohol can interfere with glycogen refueling and body fluid balance.

Part Four
For the Adventure

The Call of the Wild

by Penny Murphy

I tried not to think about water. But the harder I tried, the more I gulped. And the more I gulped, the drier my throat became.

"C'mon," I told myself. "You just had a water break 10 kilometers back. You can last another 20."

Actually, Robin and I had less than a liter of water between us and – according to the map – 37 kilometers to go before the next set of water tanks. If our information was correct, that meant nearly 25 miles on this barren south Australian plain. And even then, we had no guarantee the tanks would be full.

Unable to withstand the thirst, I guzzled the last drop of precious liquid and began counting off the kilometers. The sun blazed overhead, the dust embedded itself in my skin. Finally, I spotted a clump of vegetation alongside the road, and behind it – the tanks! But to our dismay, the "Great Water Tank Hunters" had found them before us, shooting huge holes in their bottoms. These tanks had been "dead" for a long time.

Finding water was just one of the many challenges we encountered while cycling across Australia's Nullarbor Plain, which one tourist brochure called "some of the most inhospitable, desolate country on earth."

During our 1,200-kilometer (740-mile) journey, we'd have to cope with limited supplies, inadequate shelter, hot days, freezing nights, the possibility of gale-force winds, a lack of vegetation (*nullarbor* means "treeless"), and diesel trucks or "road trains" that whizzed by at unthinkable speeds. Not exactly ideal conditions for two women cyclists.

Naturally, I was nervous about making this trip. Before leaving Norseman, the last town we'd encounter on the entire plain, I made one final effort to quell my fears. I approached the manager of a service station and told him of our plans to cycle the Eyre Highway. He eyed me as if I had a few loose springs and then "assured" me there was *nothing* between here and Ceduna, our destination. Furthermore, he advised me to register with the local police. "They'll keep an eye out for you," he said, "and if you don't turn up in a couple of years, they'll know you plum disappeared."

What does lie between Norseman and Ceduna – besides a boring, isolated, flat, barren, dry, dangerous, unsuitable-for-two-women stretch of road – are 11 gas station/roadhouses (from 65 to 200 kilometers apart) and, oh yes, a series of water tanks.

To survive under these conditions, Robin and I outfitted ourselves with an eight-day supply of food and a two-day supply of water, as well as a tent, sleeping gear, sweaters, a lantern, kerosene, and more rice and lentils than you'd ever want to eat. The only modification we made to our bikes was to put thornproof tubes in the tires.

And so, overloaded and groaning, we set out from Norseman, cycling past the town's last dwellings and entering what that same tourist brochure had called "undulating hills." With all our provisions, these undulations became knee-busters and we soon found ourselves crawling along, wondering if two weeks would ever be enough time to cross the Nullarbor. The day was perfect, though, and we were distracted by the sage-colored brush and the contrasting green and red of the gum trees. By nightfall, we had covered 110 kilometers – a surprising distance that put us more than halfway to the first gas station.

Fill 'Er Up

Just when we started thinking the Nullarbor wasn't so bad after all, it presented an unexpected threat in the form of putrid kangaroo carcasses littering the highway. These unsightly masses created a nauseating obstacle course as we pedaled toward Balladonia. For the sake of our stomachs, we learned to scan the skies for crows and wedge-tailed eagles (wingspan, eight feet) that warned of rotting 'roo.

Nevertheless, our appetites were still strong when we finally made it to Balladonia, an encouraging half-day ahead of schedule. We were anticipating fresh water, a hot pasty (Australian haute cuisine stuffed with potato and vegetables), and interesting conversation.

But nobody at the gas station paid us much attention. The girl at the snack counter was unimpressed and she reluctantly filled our jugs with 5 liters of desalinated bore water (which tastes exactly as it sounds: Yech!) and even charged us 50 cents. We made up for this budgetary infringement by taking free use of the hot shower in the women's bathroom. The water smelled like hell but it felt terrific streaming down our sweaty bodies.

Refreshed, we returned to our bikes to find a small crowd gathered around them, including two women who were "Pedaling for Peace to Perth" and some bloke who had joined them as a morale booster. They were traveling in the opposite direction and had been battling strong head winds for the last 10 days. Even with a support vehicle to carry their supplies, they were managing only 80 to 100 kilometers a day. The good news was that most of the water tanks they passed had something in them, although they couldn't remember which ones.

Considering we had few of the same luxuries, Robin and I felt like superstars as we waved goodbye. This feeling quickly subsided, however, as we came upon a set of empty water tanks 5 kilometers down the road. Knowing our supply wouldn't last too long, we pinned our hopes on the Balladonia Homestead, an old sheep station 27 kilometers away. Although it wasn't visible from the highway, we were told to look for a rusty drum and a fire hazard sign that would signal the road on which to turn.

Darkness was almost upon us when we finally found the road, but it proved to harbor a delightful encounter. Mrs. Crocker, the 90-year-old owner of the homestead, received us warmly and gave us a tour of her makeshift art gallery that included paintings of the area and its wildlife. She even invited us to sleep in the sheep-shearers' quarters, which were empty at the time. Here, we had use of a full kitchen with a gas stove and running rainwater from a tap. What a luxury! We read by candlelight as our rice and lentils stewed.

The next morning, dawn broke brilliantly over the barren landscape. There were no trees to disturb its awakening, just gentle hills and scrub brush. As the red-orange sky turned to gold and yellow, two ponies came to our door sniffing the cooking cornmeal.

We embarked on the next leg of our journey, 150 kilometers that our trusty pamphlet described as "the longest, uninterrupted, straight stretch of road in the world." Well, it may have been straight but it certainly wasn't flat. For 60 kilometers we battled an incessant uphill, which delayed our arrival at the second gas station in Caiguna.

Once there, however, our spirits were buoyed by big cans of baked beans and salmon and 5 *free* liters of boiled rainwater given us by a sympathetic roadhouse employee, who also treated us to a cup of hot chocolate. A friendly truck driver on his way to Perth even offered to deliver any supplies we might need on his return trip. (Hey, Robin. Is this the inhospitable Nullarbor? Or did we make a wrong turn somewhere?)

The "Wild" Life

So far, we'd been cycling through country that was basically wide open, sprinkled with salt brush and an occasional tree. But although we'd pedaled around hundreds of dead animals and passed numerous road signs warning of kangaroos, camels, and wombats, we had yet to see any living wildlife. No sooner did this thought cross our minds then the Nullarbor unveiled a pair of cockatoos, perched in a dead tree. Startled by our approach, they displayed their pink and white plumage while flying away. And farther along we encountered 40 to 50 kangaroos grazing by the roadside. Shy creatures, they quickly bounded off, but later we spotted several boomers – giant red 'roos – that watched us curiously before fleeing.

As we continued toward Ceduna, we became increasingly attuned to the Nullarbor. The scenery seemed to become more exciting. Maybe it was the sun or maybe it was an overdose of rice and lentils, but nearly everything caused us to stop and stare. At night, hidden from the road by underbrush, we'd lie for hours gazing at the brilliant constellations of the southern hemisphere. In fact, we exhausted our supply of flashlight batteries trying to identify them on a star chart.

One day, while perched on the brink of a delicious, 750-meter descent, we heard the whine of an approaching motorcycle. Straddling this noisy machine was a man in black "leathers," and perched on the seat – with its paws on the gas tank – was a perfectly white dog. Both driver and passenger sported matching goggles. We pinched ourselves and decided to move along before something *too* incredible happened.

The Nullarbor gave us many other surprises. One morning, again low on water, we set off into a head wind. About 25 kilometers into the ride, with threatening storm clouds overhead, we stumbled upon a pair of full water tanks. We greedily drank our fill, and then set up camp beneath their rain-catching roofs. We heated potfuls and took turns bathing behind the bushes. Suddenly, three rigs with a pair of boats in tow came roaring in, creating a cloud of dust.

"Well, look what we have here," said the first fellow to emerge, "two ladies on bicycles . . . my favorite kind." Soon our camp was inundated with six dinky, pseudo-macho Aussies, the first people we'd encountered in days.

Considering the horror stories we'd heard about Australian men, the situation seemed slightly threatening, but we put on a fresh pot of tea and offered them some. They turned out to be an amiable lot, abalone divers in search of richer territory. When they learned what we'd been subsisting on, they gave us a fresh salmon, a dozen eggs, whole-meal buns, and some milk. Hallelujah! The desert rats feast tonight!

Across This Bleak Land

By the time we reached the border of South Australia, marking the halfway point of our journey, we'd become fairly well-known. Many of the truckers who had passed us during their trips from Perth to Adelaide had relayed information on our where-abouts to other road-train pilots. In fact, people at the next road-house were expecting us.

"Oh, you're the cyclists!" exclaimed a waitress as we came in the door.

"Are we that obvious?" I whispered to Robin. Then, considering our wild, sun-bleached hair, peeling noses, and distinctive odor, I concluded that maybe we were.

The following morning we resumed our journey across the plain, heading toward the settlement of Nullarbor. Here the terrain was even more stark. There were no trees, and only infrequent patches of brush. And we began noticing signs of dingo, a type of wild dog.

With so little ground cover, it was often impossible to find shelter for the night. Once, a high-pitched whine shattered our dreams. I sat bolt upright, wide-eyed, listening to the cry of not just one, but an entire pack of dingos. And they were close. But their yowling stopped just as suddenly as it had begun, and the rest of the night was uncomfortably quiet. At dawn, I heard them again, one pack yowling to the other across the bleak land.

Almost as startling as the cry of the dingo, the flat, barren country we had been cycling through suddenly became a land of rolling hills and dense vegetation. We had entered an Aboriginal reserve with thick groves of gum trees. Although camping is illegal in these parts, we pitched our tent well off the road and hoped for the best.

Our strategy worked the first evening, but the following night we mistakenly camped too close to a local watering hole. At 2 A.M. a car pulled in, its headlights searing through our tent. My heart was pounding. The car backed off and moved another 100 meters. We heard doors slam and the soft, birdlike chatter of the Aboriginal language. They were gathering dead limbs for a fire. Minutes passed. More breaking of branches, more chatter. Somehow, I relaxed and fell back to sleep. The next morning, three bleary-eyed Aborigines drove past us, still respectful of our space.

In time, the lushness of the reserve gave way to rolling wheat fields. As we pushed closer to the thriving metropolis of Ceduna (population 3,000), the familiar signs of civilization returned – traffic, flashing lights, sidewalks, and buildings.

Cycling those last few miles into town, we felt a strong urge to remain in the wild, but the promise of fresh vegetables, yogurt, and maybe even popcorn (*anything* but rice and lentils!) lured us onward.

We had met the Nullarbor challenge – or should I say, the Nullarbor had graciously accepted two women as her guests.

Tours for Women Only

As a female cyclist, you may have experienced frustration when riding with men – and a distinct distaste for bulging quads, Lycra clothing, gear charts, and competition. To circumvent this macho atmosphere and introduce more women to cycling, several touring and adventure companies offer bicycle trips exclusively for women. Tom Horton, director of Calypso Excursions, in Newburyport, Massachusetts, started offering all-women tours in 1985 upon the recommendation of female staff members.

"Women often feel intimidated when cycling with men," he explains. "The idea behind our tours is to instill confidence."

Horton offers three-day cycling tours of Massachusetts. Each has a female leader and alternate daily routes ranging from 12 to 55 miles. The tours also include a self-discovery clinic, and mothers are even encouraged to bring their daughters.

"We're giving women an opportunity to do what they can in a group of their physical peers," says Horton.

Perhaps the oldest organization offering such tours is Woodswomen, an adventure travel firm in Minneapolis, Minnesota, that's been in operation since 1977. Among its most popular trips for women are weekend tours in Minnesota that average about 35 miles a day, and weeklong excursions in Ireland, Nova Scotia, and Mexico (approximately 50 miles a day). Director Denise Mitten – whose group also offers other types of outdoor adventure for women such as canoeing and rock climbing – says these bicycle tours usually draw from the 30- to 50-year-old age group, pulling riders who are generally looking for a good time and an easy way to meet people.

After realizing that 70 percent of his clientele was female, Dan Gray of SpokeSongs Bicycling Vacations in Mahtomedi, Minnesota, added an all-women tour for 1987. Targeted at professionals in their mid-20s to mid-40s, it's a weekend bed-and-breakfast ride that covers between 15 and 60 miles daily in

Photograph 4-1. Cycling in mixed company can be fun, but tours for women only are also available.

Minnesota and Wisconsin. Gray admits it's an experiment, but believes "there's a definite interest in active vacations for women. A lot of women on our tours are trying cycling for the first time or just getting into it."

Another organization offering exclusive bike tours is the Outdoor Woman's School in Berkeley, California. It features a two-day (50-mile) tour of the state's Big Sur Coast and a three-day (60-mile) ride among California's wineries and hot springs.

"It's like a pajama party," says the school's Carole Latimer. "Actually, there are a number of different reasons women go on these trips. Many of them are mothers who want to get away. They and their families feel better about an all-women's group."

Bonnie Bordas of Womantrek in Seattle, an adventure travel company that offers cycling tours of China and New Zealand, agrees. "The caretaking role [of being a wife or mother] is not there," she explains. "The women can be themselves."

If you're interested in taking one of these trips or in getting more information about tours for women, contact these organizations:

Calypso Excursions, Inc.
12 Federal Street
Newburyport, MA 01950
(617) 465-7173

Outdoor Woman's School/
 Call of the Wild
2519 Cedar Street
Berkeley, CA 94708
(415) 849-9292

SpokeSongs Bicycling
 Vacations
130 Fir Street, Suite B
Mahtomedi, MN 55115
(612) 429-2877

Womantrek
1411 E. Olive Way, Box 20643
Seattle, WA 98102
(206) 325-4772

Woodswomen
2550 Pillsbury Avenue S
Minneapolis, MN 55404
(612) 870-8291

Solo Touring:
One Woman's Advice

by Willamarie Huelskamp

From the seat of a bicycle, there is little difference in how a man or woman experiences the world. But there is a great disparity between the way the world treats a man by himself and the way it treats a woman cycling alone.

Maybe it's an inherent bias. For instance, when I arrived at a youth hostel in Brugge, Belgium, one fall, I was surprised to find a beautiful custom touring bike parked near the entrance. It had three water bottles, cantilevered brakes, 18 gears, and a set of well-worn panniers. I reasoned this guy must be a serious traveler to be cycling at this time of year. But while I studied the equipment, a *woman* pushed open the door and climbed on the bike. I was embarrassed by my own prejudice.

Such preconceptions are what makes solitary touring a challenge for women. Although we have some unique physical requirements, these are minor when compared with the social problems women must often overcome. In many areas, especially Third World countries and southern Europe, people are just not accustomed to seeing women touring alone. As a result, getting hassled can be an everyday occurrence. Once, in the Brecon Beacons of Wales, a truck driver pulled his rig off the road and waited as I struggled up a long, steep grade, evidently expecting me to beg him for a ride. When I rode by, ignoring him, he unleashed a string of obscenities.

Another time in the Glendale Mountains of Ireland, I was followed for two days by a man in a car. Finally, I went to the local police, who suggested I slip away by train. Good idea, I thought, only when I arrived at the Dublin station, I was approached by another guy who said, "Would you like to have relations with an Irishman?" Tell me, do male tourers have days like these?

Photograph 4-2. The world is a different place for a woman cycling alone.

Being a female cyclist can work in your favor, however – a sort of reverse discrimination. Consider the time I was cycling through Switzerland at the height of the tourist season. Even though all the campgrounds were full, the owners *always* found space for my tent. On those few occasions when a campground was not available, I'd knock on farmhouse doors. I was never turned down. And once, during a December snowstorm in Italy, I was allowed to board a baggage train for Rome while male cyclists (I later learned) were refused transportation.

When you're cycling alone, especially in Europe, you become accustomed to certain phrases repeated in a variety of languages. One often directed at me was: "All alone? What will you do if you get a puncture?" At first, I was bothered by the sexist implications of this query. But in time my irritation mellowed into indifference and, eventually, even good humor. In the Champagne region of France, I fixed a flat tire with a crowd of skeptical youths looking on. And with the help of two Dutch cyclists, I even repaired a worn-out headset. I guess what bothers me most is having to repeatedly prove myself.

There is no doubt that touring alone demands a lot of patience from a woman. But the experience of being self-sufficient builds an inner strength and confidence that can benefit you in all aspects of life. If you're considering taking a solo tour, here are a few tips to make the journey a safe and enjoyable one:

- Familiarize yourself with the customs, laws, and regions of the country you plan to visit.
- Determine what is acceptable attire for women both on and off the bike. If need be, leave the Lycra skinsuit home.
- Acquaint yourself with the language so you'll be able to understand and avoid threatening situations.
- Don't be unduly fearful of every native you meet. Answer their questions with a smile, remaining confident and polite.
- Don't broadcast that you're traveling alone.
- Know your bicycle. Pack a tool kit and repair manual.
- Be sure you have the proper equipment. I recommend a properly fitted bike, an anatomically designed women's saddle, touring shorts with a washable polyester pad, and low gears suitable for spinning.

- Bring your own supplies for menstruation since they're often unavailable along the way.
- And pack a container of Mace or some other form of self-defense just in case you meet that persistent Irishman in the train station.

Cyclewear for Women

If Marilyn Monroe wore bike shorts, she'd probably choose hot pink Lycra with *black lace* side panels.

Don't laugh – they already exist! It's the American way for every movement to have a fringe element, and in this case it's

Photograph 4-3. New fabrics make high fashion out of the most functional of women's cycling clothes.

represented by Joan Nilsen of Marin County. This bit of functional cycling lingerie is from her line of "Wombat Wear." Dawn Urbanek of San Diego has created a similarly racy short featuring tiny mirror-like dots on black Lycra.

While neither short may ever grace the gams of Olympic riders, they are indicative of the creativity and energy present in the women's cyclewear industry. Gone are the days when women had nothing to choose from but men's togs. Today, they enjoy an ever-increasing number of custom designs in a rainbow of fashionable colors.

Even established apparel companies are experimenting. "With women's clothing you can be more creative," says Amy Garbers, a designer for Cannondale. For instance, her company has introduced "leather-look black" on some of its shorts, jackets, and tights. The fabric, she explains, is heat-treated so as to create the appearance of worn or distressed leather.

Indeed, there is an ongoing revolution in women's cyclewear. But it involves function as well as fashion. For example, in designing the '88 spring line, Garbers used women racers from Team Lowery and Team Lycra as testers.

"It was real-world, trial-and-error development," she explains.

Janelle Parks of Team Lowery says it's great that Cannondale (her sponsor) is offering such clothing. "I like having a choice instead of having to custom tailor men's clothes to fit."

Women are built differently than men. Generally, they have longer legs, larger hips, and a smaller waist that's generally higher than a man's. These differences *have* to be reflected in their clothing. One area that needs special attention, for example, is the liner or chamois. Although the size of the liner is generally the same as in men's shorts, the curve is different. "Men need support and protection, while comfort is more important for a woman," says Garbers.

Elizabeth Goeke, a designer for Moving Comfort, points out that a woman's pelvic structure is wider than a man's. To accommodate this, she specifies a broader, padded liner made of French terry in a cotton/polyester blend. The cotton content, recommended by a gynecologist, has gotten a favorable reaction from most riders. Another refinement is a horizontally stitched seam, which has proven more comfortable for women than the traditional vertical seam.

Bellwether also shapes its liners specifically for women and uses a synthetic suede material padded with a thick fleecy polypropylene for wicking away moisture.

All this development is pretty startling when you consider the new era in women's cyclewear began only a few years ago. "The visibility of the cycling events in the '84 Olympics planted the seed," says Ed Dembowski of Bellwether. In addition, media coverage of cycling events and a growing acceptance of cycling as a fitness sport brought more women into bike shops. According to surveys, more than half of all new cyclists are women.

Savvy apparel manufacturers noticed this trend and began designing clothes to meet it. But at first sales lagged. Often, the new clothes were lost among the racks of men's shorts and jerseys. Dembowski's solution was to design a better rack – one that showcased the clothes with a free-standing sign and user-friendly advice. Sales for Bellwether tripled.

Nowhere is the power of choice more evident than in styles and colors. According to Goeke, although black is still the most popular color among women for cycling clothes, tastes are changing. In fact, it's possible to color-coordinate shorts, tops, and jackets.

Dembowski notes that American women don't go for the European-style "billboard look" that can sometimes make you look like a rolling advertisement. Instead, he says, clothes should be bright, active and fun, but not outlandish. According to mountain biker Jacquie Phelan, "Women's clothes have gone from mundane to downright zingy."

Part Five
Fitness Q & A

The Whys and Wherefores of Fitness

Bicycling is fitness. Ride regularly and you'll lose weight, firm muscles, and improve your cardiovascular condition. And you'll get all of these important benefits without the jarring and injuries associated with many other sports. But even though cycling is relatively easy on the body, cyclists are not immune from health problems. In fact, there are many fitness questions unique to the sport.

Here is a selection of questions from women riders. The answers are provided by *Bicycling* magazine's Fitness Advisory Board, a panel of experts in the cycling/health field.

Out of Shape

I'm approximately 50 pounds overweight and haven't been on a bike since I was a child. I'd like to start cycling for fitness and pleasure, but I have no idea where to begin. What do you suggest for a terribly out of shape 30-year-old woman? M. M., Enterprise, Ala.

Start by adopting a high-carbohydrate, low-fat diet. Omit fried foods and baked goods, add lots of fresh fruits and vegetables, and eat red meat sparingly. For further advice consult an experienced dietitian in your area.

Regarding a training program, I suggest easy riding in a low gear. Make cycling 10 miles in 1 hour your goal, and then gradually

76

increase your speed and distance (about 2 miles at a time) as you become fit. Two common mistakes made by beginners are trying to keep pace with more accomplished riders and pedaling in a gear that's too high. To avoid these pitfalls, do your own thing at your own speed. Ride about three or four times a week. Stick with this program and results will follow. *Christine L. Wells, Ph.D.*

Go Heavy on Iron

I haven't eaten red meat in six years. As an active 25-year-old female cyclist, runner, and swimmer, how can I be sure my iron requirements are being met? Stephanie Scalia, Hartford, Conn.

Lack of iron is one of the most common nutrient deficiencies in the American diet. And because of iron's role in the transport of oxygen to muscles and tissues, iron deficiency anemia can impair performance.

Good nonmeat sources of iron include dried fruit (prunes, apricots, figs), dark green leafy vegetables (spinach, mustard and turnip greens), shellfish (clams, oysters), dried beans, and whole and enriched grain products. Foods prepared in cast iron cookware can gain a significant amount of iron, especially acidic foods like tomato sauce. To increase absorption of the iron you consume, follow these simple steps:

- Include a source of vitamin C with every meal.
- If possible, eat a small amount of meat, fish, or poultry at every meal.
- Avoid drinking tea or coffee with meals.

Diane Drabinsky, R.D.

Pass on the Salt

I cycle one to two hours every day. Normally, I try to limit the amount of salt in my diet, but with all this exercise do you think I need more salt to replace what's being lost as I perspire? Debbie Foley, Newton, Mass.

Don't worry. Even in sweating off two pounds, you lose only one gram of sodium, or the equivalent of a half-teaspoon of salt (salt is 40 percent sodium). What's more, because of decreased blood volume and the conservation of sodium by the kidneys, salt concentration·actually increases during exercise. So if you were considering taking salt tablets, don't. They are unnecessary and can dangerously raise your sodium level.

There's probably more sodium in your diet than you realize. According to the National Academy of Science, your daily sodium intake should be between 1,100 and 3,300 milligrams. Most Americans consume from 3,400 to 4,600 milligrams per day. Foods such as ham, fish, cheese, corned beef, hot dogs, sausage, crackers, pretzels, popcorn, chili, canned vegetables, frozen foods, pastries, sauces, dressings, and vegetable juice contain lots of sodium. If you regularly eat such foods, you're probably getting too much sodium. Conversely, if you don't think you're meeting recommended levels, shake a bit of salt on each meal. *Diane Drabinsky, R.D.*

A Pair of Bad Knees

During the last 6 to 8 months my knees have begun to hurt – not only when I'm riding, but also when walking. The pain is in the area of the medial condyle of the femur, but occasionally radiates up and down. One doctor recommended exercising with ankle weights (this didn't work), and another said to stay off the bike (I don't want to). My bike fits me properly and I've even switched from a 13×21 freewheel to a 14×24 without success. What's a girl to do? Rachael Garrison, Corona del Mar, Calif.

I'm 36 years old and have chronic bursitis and pulled ligaments on the insides of both knees. I've had friction therapy, lidocaine injections, and long periods of rest for the past year. Yet every time I get on a bike or indoor resistance trainer, the pain returns within 24 hours. I've checked my saddle height and know all about spinning and using low gears. I'm beginning to doubt if I can ride anymore. What do you think? Meredith Kuetzman, New York, N.Y.

Photograph 5-1. Careful measurements for a well-fitted bike protect the cyclist's most important joint – the knee.

Both your ailments sound like synovial plica syndrome. A synovial plica is a nonfunctional band of tissue that runs through the knee. It's a remnant from the knee's developmental stage, and causes no problem for most people. However, the rhythmic action of cycling or running can irritate it, resulting in thickening and inflammation of the band. If you've already exhausted such conservative treatments as high saddle/high rpm cycling, medial quadriceps exercises, ice applications and anti-inflammatory medications, you might pursue an arthroscopic investigation and, perhaps, a surgical excision of your painful plica. *Andrew L. Pruitt, M.S.*

Acceptable Cholesterol

There seems to be a lot of conflicting information on "acceptable" cholesterol. Mine is 236 but my doctor hasn't sounded a warning. I'm 32 years old. I eat sensibly and have a resting pulse of 37. Do I need to reduce my cholesterol level? If so, what is acceptable? Dana N. Seelye, Wahiawa, Hawaii

I'm surprised your doctor didn't warn you. In 1984, the National Institute of Health concluded that elevated blood cholesterol is a major cause of coronary heart disease. And in 1987, the National Heart, Lung, and Blood Institute recommended that every adult be tested for cholesterol. It said levels between 200 and 239 are "borderline high."

As a borderline case, you may need treatment. Whether you do depends on if you have at least two other heart disease risk factors. These include being male, overweight, a smoker, or having high blood pressure, diabetes, or a family history of heart disease. If you do need help, a guided dietary plan is best. If this doesn't work, there's drug therapy.

Everyone should try to reduce their daily cholesterol intake to 250 to 300 milligrams. This can be achieved by limiting total dietary fat to 30 percent of your daily diet and saturated fat to 10 percent. At the same time, individuals with cholesterol problems should reduce total caloric intake and begin or increase exercise. Even if your cholesterol level isn't high, there's no advantage to becoming borderline. The lower you can get it, the better. And cycling is a perfect way to start. *Phillip W. Harvey, Ph.D.*

Sunscreen and Perspiration

I have fair skin and freckles. A doctor once warned me I was a prime candidate for skin cancer, but I'm too fond of the outdoors and my Miyata to stay inside. Over the years I've tried many sunblocks and creams, but all of them keep me from perspiring effectively. Just 15 minutes into a ride, I feel as if I'm on fire. Is there any product that will block the sun and allow me to perspire normally? Sherill Smith, Fort Worth, Tex.

Sunscreens do interfere with perspiration, but I don't know of any that inhibit it less than others. You can always use some ingenuity, however. For instance, always wear a hardshell helmet and hang a handkerchief out the back to cover your neck. Some of the new wraparound-style sunglasses shade a good portion of the face, or you can buy a helmet with a visor. Light-colored clothing will also reflect the sun and keep you cooler.

On areas that can't be covered, apply a waterproof sunscreen with the highest sun protection factor (SPF) you can find. Just a little will give you maximum protection. If you wear makeup, find a brand that contains a sunscreen. Zinc oxide reflects heat and ultraviolet light, providing a colorful coverup for sensitive areas such as the nose and lips. And to allow you to perspire more naturally, try using a little less sunscreen on the insides of arms and legs.

Remember also that ultraviolet light is prevalent even on cloudy days. There is less of it, however, in the early morning and late evenings. For people like yourself with sensitive skin, these are the safest times to ride. *David L. Smith, M.D.*

Beginning Racer

I'm a 16-year-old girl who's been cycling for 4 years and averages 10 mph. I would like to get into competitive racing, but there's hardly any news about it where I live. How can I find out about races in my area, and how should I prepare for them? Does it take a certain number of years of experience? Also, I want to buy a racing bike. Would it be smart to invest in an expensive brand? Linda Wu, Browns Mills, N.J.

In order to compete in sanctioned bicycle racing, you'll have to obtain a license from the U.S. Cycling Federation (USCF), 1750 East Boulder, Colorado Springs, CO 80909. In addition, I suggest you visit a local bicycle shop and ask about clubs in the area involved with developmental racing. You and your parents will need advice on types of racing, equipment, training, and other information. Shops and clubs can be excellent resources. If you have trouble locating a good club in your area, contact the USCF.

Photograph 5-2. Getting started in racing doesn't require an expensive bicycle.

It can put you in touch with its New Jersey representative, who can direct you to one.

I suggest your first bicycle be moderately priced since, at your age, you will most likely outgrow it. Once you've met other cyclists and raced a few times, you'll have a better idea of how to upgrade your equipment. You're lucky that you've discovered cycling at a young age. You can look forward to many years of improvement and enjoyment. *Edmund R. Burke, Ph.D.*

After a Century

I'm a 45-year-old woman who recently resumed cycling after a 10-year hiatus. I'm training for a century but I don't want to lose my conditioning after the event. How much cycling should I do postcentury to keep what I've gained? Must I continue to ride 6 days a week, as I do now, or will a few less do the trick? Nancy Kay, Tucson, Ariz.

How you train after a century depends on what you want to accomplish. If you're just out to maintain fitness, you can reduce your riding. Research indicates that less training is required to maintain cardiovascular fitness once a certain level is attained. You can probably do this by riding 20 miles or 75 minutes (whichever comes first) three to four times per week at high cadence, with an occasional 50-mile ride. If, on the other hand, you want to keep improving your century times *and* your fitness, you'll need to continue training at precentury levels or higher. *Christine L. Wells, Ph.D.*

Starting Out

I'm 15 years old and recently became very interested in racing. The salesman at my local shop helped me choose the right bike, but I need training advice. Can you help me? Julie Smith, Burke, Va.

First, master the basics of proper technique: Learn to ride a straight line and concentrate on pedaling or "spinning" at a high cadence (90 to 110 rpm).

Next, build your mileage base. Start the season slowly with a few short rides to gain fitness. When you're able to ride four or more times a week, gradually increase the distance of your long ride to at least twice the mileage of your regular training rides (i.e., if you ride 15 miles on weekdays, try going 30 on Saturday or Sunday).

After you've built a solid base (about one-third of your estimated yearly mileage), incorporate some hillwork or interval training into your schedule once or twice a week. Find a hill you can climb without exhausting yourself. After a sufficient warm-up, climb the hill, recover on the way down, and then go up again for a second interval. As your fitness improves, add more repeats.

Intervals develop speed. They can range from structured $\frac{1}{4}$-, $\frac{1}{2}$-, or 1-mile repeats to random sprints between telephone poles along a fairly flat road. Again, begin with an easy warm-up and gradually increase the number of sprints. End each session with an easy ride home. By following these suggestions, you'll be logging quality miles that build power, speed, and endurance. *Kate Delhagen*

Speed or Distance?

I'm a new rider who cycles to firm my legs, lose weight, and stay healthy. I ride 15 to 20 miles four or five days a week. To reach my goals should I be riding for speed or distance? And should I be cycling every day? Sherri Sharpe, Leesburg, Ga.

Yours is a common question. Firming muscles, losing weight, and staying healthy are three major reasons people exercise. To realize such goals you need to ride for speed *and* distance. Your training week should contain these three components:

Moderate days. To stay trim, forget about the clock and ride moderate distances at a comfortable pace. For you, this will entail two or three 15-mile rides per week.

Endurance days. To improve your stamina, go on one long ride every week. For you, this might be 40 to 60 miles. Once again, don't worry about time. Your goal should be to complete the distance.

Speed days. These are crucial to cardiovascular improvement and muscle tone. Twice a week, try to complete 15 miles in an hour while maintaining a cadence of 85 to 90 rpm. Gradually increase the speed and distance as you become fitter.

This schedule, which allows for at least one day of rest each week, will bring you all the benefits cycling has to offer. *Christine L. Wells, Ph.D.*

Upper-Body Strength

I'm a 31-year-old woman who's been cycling a short distance to and from work for several years. Last summer I began to ride more often, primarily to develop my fitness. By the fall, I was doing at least one 50-mile ride every weekend. The only problem I've encountered while making the transition from casual commuter to fitness rider is that my upper body seems much weaker than my legs, and on rides longer than 20 miles my shoulders and arms become so tired I can barely steer. What's the best way to prevent my upper body from becoming stiff, sore, and achy during long rides? M. B., Washington, D.C.

Photograph 5-3. Weights build strength where women need it most – the upper body.

Cyclists are notorious for having weak upper bodies. Many times the legs and heart are capable of pedaling long distances, but the arms and shoulders refuse to cooperate. The trick? Strengthen your upper body without adding bulk.

By incorporating some form of resistance training into your weekly routine, you'll develop the strength to enjoy long rides. First, decide whether you want a simple, at-home strength training program, or one devised for you by a professional at a local health club.

If you choose the at-home approach, you won't need to buy any fancy equipment. Just use your own body weight as resistance. The best upper-body strength builders are push-ups, pull-ups, and tricep dips (get between two tables or chairs, place a hand on each, and slowly lower and raise yourself). To build mid-body strength, crucial for maintaining good riding position, do a few sets of abdominal crunches (lie on your back with hands across your chest, curl up slightly until your head and shoulders are 6 inches off the floor, hold 3 to 5 seconds while your abdominal muscles tighten), and back extensions (on your stomach, hands on buttocks, slowly lift your head and shoulders from the floor and hold 3 to 5 seconds as your lower back muscles tighten). If you have a barbell, do bench presses, military presses, and arm curls.

At a health club, machines allow you to safely perform a variety of exercises. Ask an instructor to demonstrate several upper-body machines, and don't be afraid to try new exercises.

Regardless of your methods, the key to building strength for

Photograph 5-4. A strong back is a pain-free back.

Photograph 5-5. Weights can put *you* in charge.

cycling is to perform numerous repetitions with light to moderate weights. After a few weeks of training every other day, your strength should be significantly improved. But remember to keep riding so your leg strength doesn't lag. *Kate Delhagen*

Exercise-Induced Asthma

I'm a 28-year-old woman who started cycling about a year ago. Whenever I ride hard for more than a few minutes my chest gets tight and I have trouble breathing. Often, this persists for several hours after a ride. Is this exercise-induced asthma? If so, is there anything I can do to counteract it? Nancy Jaster, Englewood, Colo.

Your symptoms could stem from exercise-induced asthma. I suggest asking your doctor for a device known as an *albuterol metered-dose inhaler*. If it relieves your symptoms, then exercise-induced asthma is, indeed, your problem. You'll have to continue using the inhaler, though. If it doesn't help, see your physician for further examination. *David L. Smith, M.D.*

Pack Makes Her Panic

For some reason, whenever I ride with more than two cyclists, I get nervous. Do you have any suggestions for overcoming this fear? Maria Musciano, Somerdale, N.J.

To ride in traffic, whether among motorists or other cyclists, you must be relaxed, confident, and in control of your bike. If you have a tense upper body and a death grip on the handlebars, you won't be able to ride a straight line. Keep your elbows bent and your grip moderately tight. If you begin to get nervous, take a few deep breaths. And remember that how much control you have over your bike also depends on how well it fits – so have this checked.

The more often you ride with a group, the less nervous you'll feel. Join a touring club and attend its weekend group rides. Practice your paceline riding with those riders who seem the smoothest. Start by staying one bike length from the rider in front, then gradually close the gap as you become more confident of your abilities. Watch the road past the rider's shoulder or legs, rather than staring at the wheel. In time, you should be riding within a wheel's length and enjoying the effects of drafting. *John Kukoda*

Pain behind the Knee

During the winter, I did more weight training than riding. Now that I'm cycling again, I've started experiencing knee pain – a stiffness and soreness behind the kneecap. When I straighten the leg, the bone feels as if it's shifting or slipping. What can I do to ease this problem? Susan Evans, Dallas, Tex.

Although pain in the back of the knee is less common than pain about the kneecap, it's just as frustrating to diagnose. Two things may be causing your problem: (1) your saddle is too high, causing you to overextend your knee at the bottom of each pedal stroke; or (2) you may have a more serious problem called a Baker's cyst. This is a bulging of the posterior knee capsule (the tight elastic bag around the joint), caused by the overproduction of synovial fluid. Since such fluid is usually produced in response to some internal derangement of the knee, I'd suggest seeing a sports medicine therapist. *Andrew L. Pruitt, M.S.*

Earaches

Every time I ride when it's cool or windy, I get an earache. Do you have any suggestions for preventing this? Barb Lepsoe, Burnaby, British Columbia, Canada

Sometimes traditional remedies can't be beat. Filling your ears with cotton is still the best way to prevent earaches. It's not known why cold and wind cause earaches in some people, but it may be due to cooling of the eardrum. Those with large ear canals and little earwax seem to have the most trouble. To minimize your problem, use cotton before every ride and don't clean the wax from your ears with swabs or drops. *David L. Smith, M.D.*

Numb Toes

Why do my toes fall asleep or become numb after only a few miles of riding? Several years ago I tried cycling shoes but didn't like them because my feet got hot. Now I ride with tennis shoes. Any suggestions? Donna Ruesch, Lakeland, Fl.

Toe numbness is usually caused by compression and irritation of the foot's digital nerves. This is often the resu t of shoes that are too short and/or narrow. In addition, a tennis shoe does not protect the metatarsal head (the ball) of the foot from the pedal, and this can cause irritation. It's also possible that you have a condition known as neuroma (a benign growth among the nerves), which can be aggravated by ill-fitting shoes. My advice is to change to an appropriate cycling shoe, whether the cleated or touring type. Make sure the shoe is the proper size for your foot. If this doesn't help, try reducing some of the pressure on the ball of the foot by putting a ¼-inch felt pad, called a metatarsal pad, just behind it. If the numbness persists, see a podiatrist. *Mitchell L. Feingold, D.P.M.*

Ruptured Disc

I'm a 29-year-old female who has been cycling for approximately five years. Recently I had surgery for a ruptured disc (lumbar 4-5). Prior to this, I switched from a sport/touring to a racing frame, and from a 12×28 to a 12×24 freewheel. A friend who made similar changes also ruptured her disc. Does our cycling have anything to do with our injuries? Deborah J. Brown, Jamestown, N.Y.

It is doubtful that cycling had anything to do with the ruptured vertebral discs. A ruptured disc is the herniation of the cushioning material between the vertebra, sometimes putting pressure on the spinal cord. Cycling and other non-heel-strike sports should continue to be your activities of choice.

Improper bike fit that makes you extend your back to reach the handlebar can cause back pain. Overgearing can make you drive harder with the hip, which can produce low back pain and spasms. And the steeper angles which make your racing bike more responsive probably make it less comfortable – but none of these would cause disc problems.

In fact, cycling is often used during convalescence from disc injuries. My only biomechanical suggestion would be to raise your handlebar stem so you're in a more upright position, thereby eliminating stress on the low back. Then, as your back strengthens, gradually return to a more efficient cycling postion. *Andrew L. Pruitt, M.S.*

The Best Gear for Climbing

I'm a 50-year-old woman who rides for fun and exercise. When climbing, I get off the saddle and pedal in a high gear. I've noticed other riders spin uphill in a low gear. Which way is best? Sue Larsen, Hinton, Iowa

You pose an excellent question. Unfortunately, the answer is not known. In fact, I'm currently researching this subject. While it's too early to discuss preliminary findings, I can comment on the nature of the problem.

The key question is whether standing on the pedals affords any mechanical advantage in generating force. I don't know yet, although I hope to find out. I do know that conquering hills in a high gear often develops at least one part of a cyclist: the ego. Having a small freewheel is often considered a measure of a rider's ability and strength. For this superficial reason, many cyclists prefer to stand while climbing. For some individuals this works fine, but for others a steady spin is the answer.

To discover what's right for you, try climbing the same hill several times. Use a different gear each time, but always ride at the same speed. Then ask yourself these questions: Which gear seemed easiest? Which one produced the lowest (most efficient) heart rate? And did pushing the higher gears hurt my knees?

The answers will determine what's best for your personal climbing style. *David P. Swain, Ph.D.*

Credits

The information in this book is drawn from these and other articles from *Bicycling* magazine.

"Introduction" Connie Carpenter Phinney, "Just a Girl on a Bike," *Bicycling,* August 1987, p. 53.

"Can a Woman Be an Exceptional Cyclist?" Gretchen Reynolds, "Fast and Feminine," *Bicycling,* August 1987, pp. 54-57.

"Five Myths" Renee Russak, "Women on Wheels," *Bicycling,* June 1988, pp. 56-62.

"Bicycles for Women" John Kukoda, "Short and Sweet," *Bicycling,* August 1987, p. 58.

"The Proper Fit" John Kukoda, "Sitting Pretty," *Bicycling,* April 1987, pp. 146-153.

"Fit Tips for Small Riders" John Kukoda, "Make Your Bike Fit Better," *Bicycling,* August 1987, p. 80.

"Learning the Lingo" Nelson Pena, "New Rider: Learning the Lingo," *Bicycling,* August 1987, p. 84.

"Weekly Bike Maintenance" Don Cuerdon, "Repair Stand: Weekly Maintenance," *Bicycling,* April 1988, pp. 104-105.

"The Best Riding Tips I Know" Connie Carpenter Phinney and Mark Gorski, "The Best Riding Tips I Know," *Bicycling,* June 1988, pp. 46-54.

"Five More Training Tips" Fred Matheny, "Be Your Own Coach," *Bicycling,* April 1987, p. 65.

"Meals for the Miles" Nelson Pena, "What Does This Man Know That You Don't?" *Bicycling,* July 1988, pp. 72-77.

"Different Rides, Different Diets" Liz Applegate, Ph.D., "Different Rides, Different Diets," *Bicycling,* July 1988, pp. 78-80.

"The Call of the Wild" Penny Murphy, "The Call of the Wild," *Bicycling,* June 1986, pp. 98-105.

"Tours for Women Only" Patricia Lynch, "Tours for Women Only," *Bicycling,* August 1987, p. 78.

"Solo Touring: One Woman's Advice" Willamarie Huelskamp, "A Woman Alone," *Bicycling,* June 1986, pp. 102-103.

"Cyclewear for Women" Liz Fritz and Dave Sellers, "Women's Wear," *Bicycling,* June 1988, pp. 64-70.

"The Whys and Wherefores of Fitness" "Fitness Q&A," *Bicycling,* December 1987 to July 1988.

Photographs

Angelo Caggiano: photos 3-1, 3-2, 3-3, 3-4, 3-5, 3-6; Jim Cassimus: photo 1-3; Mark Clifford: photo 1-1; T. L. Gettings: photo 1-2; John P. Hamel: photo 4-1; Donna Hornberger: photo 3-7; Ed Landrock: photos 2-1, 2-2, 4-2, 5-1; Christie C. Tito: photos 3-8, 4-3, 5-2; Sally Shenk Ullman: photos 5-3, 5-4, 5-5.